Cooking With Children Made Easy

Fun, Safe, and Simple!

Kristine Burns

Table of Contents

Introduction:

Cooking in the Kitchen With

Children

Have you ever tried inviting your child to cook with you?

Children really like it when their parents allow them to do "grownup" tasks, especially at home. Cooking is an excellent example of a task that children really enjoy doing. Cooking with your child is a wonderful way to spend quality time with them while teaching them some valuable skills and concepts. And the best part is, you always get something tasty to share after each cooking session!

Benefits of Cooking With Kids

For grownups, cooking is simply a chore that needs to be done so they have something to eat. But for children, cooking is a fascinating experience that involves a lot of fun things. As a parent, you can awaken your child's love of cooking by inviting them to cook different dishes with you. Aside from this, cooking with kids comes with many other benefits:

- Gives you plenty of opportunities to teach them about healthy foods and why these foods are good for them.

- Allows your child to learn different concepts. For instance, measuring and counting ingredients are math concepts. Learning the names of ingredients and the different processes involved in cooking builds their vocabulary. Following the steps in recipes improves their comprehension and sequencing. These are just some examples of how cooking can help your child learn academic concepts that they will also learn in school.

- It's an excellent way for them to explore the world using their different senses. They can listen to different sounds, smell different scents, touch different textures, see everything around the kitchen, and taste different foods.

- Learning new skills and practicing those skills through hands-on activities makes your child feel more confident in themselves.

- Following different recipes and even experimenting with different ingredients enhances your child's creative thinking.

- Explaining the importance of following the steps in recipes teaches your child the importance of following directions. This also teaches your child to be responsible, especially if you allow them to start following recipes on their own.

It also becomes easier for you to encourage your child to try new dishes when they helped prepare and cook those dishes. This would make mealtime a lot easier for both of you!

Safety Guidelines

While cooking can be a fun and exciting activity for children, it comes with a number of risks. From hot stoves to sharp knives and everything in between, there are a lot of things in your kitchen that could cause harm to your child. So, if you want your child to learn how to cook properly, you need to focus on safety. Here are the most important safety rules and reminders to teach your child while cooking:

- Start by setting the basic safety rules of the kitchen. Focus on the basics like washing hands before and after cooking, never starting to cook without you or any other adult present in the kitchen, and no playing or running around while cooking. Then you can move on to the other kitchen rules and guidelines as you go along.

- Name everything in your kitchen and point out which items they can touch or use and which ones are off-limits. Explain why your child isn't allowed to touch or use those things without your supervision.

- Dress your child appropriately. Tie long hair, let them wear an apron, and have other apparel such as oven mitts ready, depending on the recipe.

- Before you start cooking, go through the recipe with your child. Prepare all of the ingredients and items or equipment you will use, then remind your child again which items they can use or touch. Also, explain which steps in the recipe are for your child and which ones should be done by you or with your help.

- Always keep the kitchen clean, especially the areas where you prepare food. The same thing applies to all of the tools and equipment you will use to avoid contamination of any kind.

- Teach your child how to use kitchen tools, equipment, and appliances properly and safely. Demonstrate how to use everything, then supervise your child until you see that they have learned how to do or use things correctly.

- Whenever something spills, wipe it up right away to avoid accidents. Cleanup should always be a part of the process, so you need to teach your child how to do this too.

Always communicate with your child while you are cooking with them. Talk to them about the ingredients you use, the preparation methods, cooking processes, measuring, and so on. Explaining everything to your child will make them aware of everything that's happening in the kitchen, which would make them more engaged in the process.

Chapter 1:

Let's Get Started

Are you excited to start cooking with your child?

You're almost there! Before we move on to the recipes, you need to prepare your kitchen first. In itself, cooking can be a complicated process. To make it simpler and more enjoyable for your child, it's a good idea to plan each cooking sessions in advance and prepare your kitchen to make it safe for your child.

Setting up the Kitchen

Whenever you cook in the kitchen, you move with confidence and grace since you already know what you're doing, and you know exactly where everything is. But if you have ever tried cooking in a kitchen that's unfamiliar to you, you may feel a bit confused and overwhelmed.

Your child may feel the same way when they first step into your kitchen to cook.

But if you can set up your kitchen to make it suitable for your child, they will feel happy, confident, and comfortable whenever you want to cook with them. Here are some kitchen-organizing tips for you:

- When arranging the items in your kitchen, make sure that the items your child is allowed to use are all within their reach. This will make it easier for them to learn how to move independently in your kitchen as you keep cooking with them regularly.

- Place labels on the items in your kitchen that you will frequently be using when you cook together. Keep the labels on the items until your child is already familiar with everything that you use.

- Prepare a workstation for your child in the kitchen. Whenever you cook with them, make sure to set everything up in that area.

- Make sure your kitchen is always clean, and make it a habit to clean up after cooking and even while cooking, if possible.

- If you can, invest in child-sized and child-friendly kitchen items to make their cooking experiences more enjoyable. Using items that are meant for children could also make your child feel more confident when learning cooking tasks.

- Add some visual aids to your kitchen, such as posters with pictures of the basic kitchen rules like washing hands, wearing the right clothes while cooking, making sure there is always an adult present, and more.

After setting up your kitchen, explain to your child that cooking should only be done in the kitchen to make sure that every meal that's made is clean and safe to eat. Also, remind your child that they are only allowed to use and touch certain items in the kitchen, the ones that you have placed within their reach.

Essential Cooking Tools for Kids

Cooking with your child can be a lot of fun, but it can also be a messy task. Expect your child to experiment with different things, especially when you start including them in the kitchen when you're cooking. After setting up your kitchen to make it suitable for your child, you also need to prepare the basic kitchen equipment that you will need each time you want to follow a recipe with your child. Here are some of the basic kitchen items you can start preparing or investing in:

- an apron for your child to wear every time you cook with them.

- for baking, you need measuring spoons, measuring cups, piping bags, cookie cutters of different shapes and sizes, a strainer, a baking tray, a baking sheet, a pie pan, a whisk, and a rolling pin.

- bowls and plates of different sizes.

- serving bowls and serving plates.

- a set of knives, a peeler, and a chopping board.

- a step stool for your child to stand on while they do kitchen tasks or while washing their hands or dishes in the sink.

- pots, pans, and skillets.

- oven and microwave-safe containers.

- airtight containers and mason jars for storing the food that you cook or for storing leftovers to prevent spoilage.

You don't have to buy these things all at the same time. Start with the items you already have in your kitchen, then gradually buy more things over time, whenever you have the budget for it. Whenever you have something new, introduce it to your child, and show them how to use it too.

Overview of Basic Ingredients

Whenever you follow a recipe, you need to prepare all of the ingredients needed. While you can buy the necessary ingredients for your recipe before cooking it, stocking your kitchen and pantry with basic ingredients is a good idea too. That way, whenever you or your child wants to cook something, you will always have basic ingredients to work with:

- dry spices like pepper, salt, oregano, cinnamon, turmeric, cornstarch, and paprika

- other dry ingredients like pasta, rice, quinoa, breadcrumbs, oats, and sugar

- dairy products like yogurt, cheese, milk, butter, and cream

- produce that doesn't spoil easily, like garlic, onions, potatoes, carrots, lemons, and some types of fresh herbs

- condiments like ketchup, mayonnaise, vinegar, soy sauce, peanut butter, and honey

- different types of oil

- canned goods like chickpeas, beans, stock, and tomatoes

- baking basics like flour, chocolate chips, cocoa powder, yeast, baking powder, baking soda, syrup, and rainbow sprinkles

Just make sure to check the expiry dates of any food items you have at home before using them in your dishes. Also, avoid keeping foods that spoil easily to prevent food waste. But with these basic ingredients, you can easily cook different dishes at any time of the day!

Chapter 2:

Simple Breakfast Delights

Breakfast is the most important meal of the day. We all need energy to get through our mornings, and we can get that energy from a delicious and nutritious meal. The great thing about breakfast is that there are so many dishes to choose from. Check out these recipes that you can easily cook and prepare with your child.

Pancake Palooza

Classic Pancakes

Pancakes are a classic breakfast treat and there are many ways to cook them. Here is the simplest recipe out there, which is the perfect way to introduce breakfast delights to your child.

Time: *15 minutes*

Serving Size: *4 servings*

Prep Time: *5 minutes*

Cook Time: *10 minutes*

Ingredients:

- 1/4 tsp salt (fine)

- 1/4 tsp vanilla extract

- 1 tsp butter (unsalted, melted)

- 1/2 tbsp baking powder

- 1/2 tbsp sugar

- 3/4 cup of flour

- 3/4 cup of milk

- 1 egg

- cooking spray

Directions:

1. In a bowl, add the flour, sugar, baking powder, and salt, then mix well.

2. In another bowl, add the butter, egg, vanilla extract, and milk, then mix well.

3. Use your fingers to create a well in the middle of the bowl with the dry ingredients, then pour the wet ingredient mixture into it.

4. Set your electric mixer on low and mix all the ingredients until well combined.

5. Use cooking spray to lightly grease a pan, then place it on the stove over medium-high heat.

6. When the pan is hot, pour 1/4 cup of batter into it.

7. Cook the pancake until you see small bubbles all over the surface.

8. Flip the pancake over, then continue cooking for about 1 minute.

9. Transfer the cooked pancake to a plate, then repeat the cooking steps until you have used up all of the pancake batter.

10. Serve the pancakes while warm with your child's favorite toppings.

Pancake Lion

Make pancakes even more appealing to your child by using them to create tasty and cute masterpieces. Here is a recipe for a pancake lion using the same pancake recipe as the one above.

Time: *10 minutes*

Serving Size: *1 serving*

Prep Time: *10 minutes*

Cook Time: *no cooking time*

Ingredients:

- 1/3 of a very small pancake (cut in half)

- 1 large pancake

- 1 raspberry

- 1 small pancake

- 2 very small pancakes

- 2 almond slices

- 2 banana slices

- 2 blueberries

- 4 strawberries (sliced lengthwise into 4 slices)

- chocolate hazelnut spread

Directions:

1. Use the large pancake, small pancake, and very small pancakes to make the face of the lion.

2. Place the very small pancake halves on top to make the ears, then spread some chocolate hazelnut in the middle of each ear.

3. Surround the large pancake with strawberry slices to make the mane.

4. Use banana slices, almond slices, and blueberries to make the eyes.

5. Place the raspberry in the middle for the nose.

6. Enjoy!

Berry Cheesecake Pancakes

Adding berries and other fresh fruits to pancakes will make them tastier and healthier. You can add these fruits as toppings along with other tasty treats like in this recipe.

Time: 20 *minutes*

Serving Size: 2 *servings*

Prep Time: 10 *minutes*

Cook Time: 10 *minutes*

Ingredients:

- 1/2 tbsp icing sugar

- 1/2 tbsp maple syrup

- 1/8 cup of almonds (roughly chopped)

- 1/4 cup of cream cheese

- 1/3 cup of blueberries (fresh or frozen)

- 2 ginger cookies (crushed)

- 2 pancakes (follow the first recipe for Classic Pancakes)

Directions:

1. Prepare the pancakes by following the recipe for Classic Pancakes. You will need 2 pancakes for each person in this recipe. After cooking, set the pancakes aside.

2. In a saucepan, add the maple syrup and blueberries over low heat. Cook for about 3 minutes until syrupy and soft.

3. Add the icing sugar and cream cheese, then mix well.

4. Spoon the syrupy toppings over the pancakes, then top with crushed cookies and chopped almonds.

5. Serve immediately.

Choco Chip Pancakes

Children love chocolate chip cookies, and if you tell your child that you will be adding chocolate chips to their fluffy pancakes, they will surely feel excited.

Time: *15 minutes*

Serving Size: *2 servings*

Prep Time: *5 minutes*

Cook Time: *10 minutes*

Ingredients:

- 1/2 tsp baking powder

- 1 1/2 tbsp caster sugar

- 1/3 cup of chocolate chips

- 2/3 cup of whole milk

- 3/4 cup of self-rising flour

- 1 egg

- salt

- butter (for cooking)

- whipped cream (for serving)

Directions:

1. In a sieve, add the baking powder, flour, and a pinch of salt, then sift the ingredients into a bowl.

2. Add the caster sugar and mix well to combine.

3. In a jug, add the milk and egg, then whisk well.

4. Use your finger to make a well in the middle of the flour ingredient mixture, then pour the milk mixture into the well.

5. Use a whisk to gently combine the wet and dry ingredients until you get a smooth pancake batter.

6. Fold the chocolate chips into the batter.

7. In a pan, add some butter over medium heat, then swirl it around to coat the bottom.

8. When the butter is hot, pour 3 tablespoons of batter into it.

9. Cook for about 1 to 2 minutes until you see bubbles on the surface of the pancake.

10. Use a spatula to flip over the pancake, then continue cooking for about 2 minutes.

11. Transfer the pancake to a plate, then repeat the same steps until you use up all of the pancake batter.

12. Divide the pancakes between two plates.

13. Top each stack with whipped cream and serve.

Vegan Pancakes

If you want to introduce your child to plant-based foods or if they have certain food allergies that prevent them from eating certain ingredients, you can try whipping up these vegan pancakes with them.

Time: 20 *minutes*

Serving Size: 2 *servings*

Prep Time: 10 *minutes*

Cook Time: 10 *minutes*

Ingredients:

- 1/2 tsp baking powder

- 1/2 tsp vanilla extract

- 1/2 tsp cinnamon

- 1/4 cup of wholemeal spelt flour

- 1/2 cup of plant-based yogurt

- 1/3 cup of soy milk

- rapeseed oil (for cooking)

- 1 tbsp pecans (chopped, for serving)

- 1/3 cup of strawberries (stems removed, sliced, for serving)

Directions:

1. In a bowl, add the baking powder, flour, and cinnamon, baking powder, then whisk well.

2. In a jug, add the yogurt, vanilla extract, and soy milk, then mix well.

3. Use your finger to make a well in the middle of the flour mixture, then pour the yogurt mixture into the well.

4. Use a whisk to gently combine the wet and dry ingredients until you get a thick pancake batter.

5. Lightly grease a pan with rapeseed oil, then place it over medium heat.

6. When the oil is hot enough, pour 3 tablespoons of batter into it.

7. Cook for about 1 to 2 minutes until you see bubbles on the surface of the pancake.

8. Use a spatula to flip over the pancake, then continue cooking for about 2 minutes.

9. Transfer the pancake to a plate, then repeat the same steps until you use up all of the pancake batter.

10. Divide the pancakes between 2 plates.

11. Top with pecans and berries, then serve.

Fruit Parfait Creations

Yogurt and Berries

Berries go so well with yogurt in parfaits because their flavors blend together so well. If your little one loves to eat berries, they will surely have fun with this recipe.

Time: *5 minutes*

Serving Size: *2 servings*

Prep Time: *5 minutes*

Cook Time: *no cooking time*

Ingredients:

- 1 tbsp honey

- 1/8 cup graham crackers (crushed)

- 1/8 cup of walnuts (finely chopped)

- 1/2 cup of mixed berries (fresh, washed, chopped)

- 1/2 cup of yogurt (Greek or plain)

Directions:

1. Prepare all of the ingredients by placing them in individual bowls.

2. With your child, layer the ingredients in parfait glasses until you reach the top.

3. Serve immediately or chill in the refrigerator before serving.

Mixed Fruits and Yogurt

This fruity parfait recipe is so simple and easy that your child might be able to do it after preparing it with you for the first time. The best part is that it's super customizable too!

Time: *10 minutes*

Serving Size: *2 servings*

Prep Time: *10 minutes*

Cook Time: *no cooking time*

Ingredients:

- 2 tbsp almonds (toasted, sliced)

- 1/2 cup of strawberries (stems removed, sliced)

- 1/2 cup of cantaloupe (chopped)

- 1/2 cup of kiwi (peeled, sliced)

- 1/2 banana (sliced)

- 1 cup of yogurt (low-fat, vanilla flavor)

Directions:

1. Add layers of fruit and yogurt into 2 parfait glasses. You can either add layers of fruit separately or mix them all together in a bowl and alternate layers of mixed fruits and yogurt.

2. Top each glass with sliced almonds and serve.

Yogurt With Fruity Fillings

The great thing about parfaits is that you can use different ingredients based on your child's preferences. Here is another version with fruity fillings and other toppings.

Time: 10 *minutes*

Serving Size: 2 *servings*

Prep Time: 2 *servings*

Cook Time: *no cooking time*

Ingredients:

- 2 tsp honey

- 1/2 cup of toppings like sliced almonds, crushed pistachios, granola, chopped walnuts, chia seeds, or sesame seeds

- 1 cup of sliced fruit like berries, pineapple, kiwi, mango, bananas, cherries, peaches, figs, or even stewed apples

- 1 cup of yogurt

Directions:

1. Spoon layers of yogurt, fruits, and toppings into 2 parfait glasses until you reach the top.

2. Drizzle each parfait with honey and serve.

Rainbow Fruits

There is nothing more appealing to children than colorful food. Make your child feel more excited about eating parfaits by using ingredients with all colors of the rainbow.

Time: 10 *minutes*

Serving Size: 2 *servings*

Prep Time: 10 *minutes*

Cook Time: *no cooking time*

Ingredients:

- 1/4 cup of blueberries (fresh, washed)

- 1/4 cup of strawberries (stems removed, sliced)

- 1/4 cup pineapple (chopped)

- 1/2 cup of Greek yogurt (vanilla flavor)

- 1/4 cup red grapes (seedless)

- 1 kiwi (peeled, chopped)

- 1 mandarin (peeled, segmented)

Directions:

1. Start by adding layers of fruit into 2 parfait glasses following the colors of the rainbow.

2. Top each parfait glass with yogurt and serve.

Fully-Loaded

Parfaits can be eaten right away or chilled first, then eaten as a dessert or a snack. Either way, this parfait will surely fill you up in a very nice, satisfying way.

Time: *10 minutes*

Serving Size: *2 servings*

Prep Time: *10 minutes*

Cook Time: *no cooking time*

Ingredients:

- 1 tsp coconut flakes

- 1/4 cup of mixed berries (fresh, washed)

- 1 tsp vanilla extract

- 2 tbsp pecans (sliced)

- 3/4 cup of Greek yogurt

- 3 tbsp almond butter

- 1/4 cup of heavy whipping cream

Directions:

1. In a bowl, add the heavy cream, vanilla extract, and yogurt, then whisk well.

2. Add layers of fresh fruits and the yogurt mixture to 2 parfait glasses.

3. Top each parfait glass with almond butter and serve.

Easy Omelet Adventures

Cheese and Veggies

Adding veggies to your child's diet can sometimes be challenging. But with recipes like these, your little one might start feeling excited about having vegetables in their meals.

Time: *15 minutes*

Serving Size: *3 servings*

Prep Time: *5 minutes*

Cook Time: *10 minutes*

Ingredients:

- 1/2 tsp oregano (dried)

- 2 eggs

- 1 small tomato (seeds removed, diced)

- 1/8 cup of cheddar cheese (grated)

- butter (for frying)

Directions:

1. In a pan, add some butter over medium heat.

2. When the butter is hot, add the oregano and tomato. Cook for about 2 to 3 minutes.

3. Transfer the veggies to a plate and use a paper towel to wipe the pan clean.

4. In a bowl, add the eggs and whisk them together.

5. Add more butter to the pan, then place it over low heat.

6. When it's hot enough, pour the eggs in.

7. Cook the eggs until they are just about set.

8. Sprinkle the omelet with cheese, tomato, and oregano.

9. Use a spatula to lift one side of the omelet, then fold it over. Continue cooking until the eggs have set.

10. Transfer the omelet to a plate and serve while hot.

Meat, Cheese, and Veggies

Adding meat to omelets will make them more savory and appealing to children. You can add different types of meat depending on what your child really loves.

Time: *15 minutes*

Serving Size: *2 servings*

Prep Time: *5 minutes*

Cook Time: *10 minutes*

Ingredients:

- 1/4 tsp black pepper

- 1/4 tsp kosher salt

- 1 tsp water

- 1/4 cup of sausage (sliced, cooked)

- 1/4 cup of spinach

- 1/2 cup of cheddar cheese (shredded)

- 3 eggs

- butter (for cooking)

Directions:

1. In a skillet, add some butter over medium heat.

2. In a bowl, add the eggs, salt, pepper, and water, then whisk until fluffy and light.

3. When the butter is hot, pour the egg mixture into it.

4. Cook the eggs until they are just set.

5. Sprinkle the sausage slices, spinach leaves, and cheese over the omelet.

6. Use a spatula to lift one side of the omelet, then fold it over. Continue cooking until the eggs have set.

7. Transfer the omelet to a plate and serve immediately.

Savory Bacon

Bacon is so tasty and versatile that you can add it to different dishes. Making a bacon omelet is probably one of the tastiest ways to cook this simple dish.

Time: *15 minutes*

Serving Size: *2 servings*

Prep Time: *5 minutes*

Cook Time: *10 minutes*

Ingredients:

- 1/4 cup of sharp cheddar cheese (shredded)

- 2 slices of bacon (cooked, diced)

- 3 eggs

- pepper

- salt

- butter (for cooking)

Directions:

1. In a pan, add some butter over medium heat.

2. In a bowl, add the eggs, salt, and pepper, then whisk to combine.

3. When the butter is hot, pour the egg mixture into it.

4. Cook the eggs until they are just set.

5. Sprinkle the diced bacon and cheddar cheese over the omelet.

6. Use a spatula to lift one side of the omelet, then fold it over. Continue cooking until the eggs have set.

7. Transfer the omelet to a plate and serve while hot.

Super Cheesy

Cheese omelets are easy, simple, and super tasty. Add one type of cheese like in this recipe, or make it even more interesting by combining different types of cheeses.

Time: 15 minutes

Serving Size: 2 servings

Prep Time: 5 minutes

Cook Time: 10 minutes

Ingredients:

- 1 tbsp milk

- white pepper

- 1/4 cup of Emmental cheese (shredded)

- 3 eggs

- salt

- butter (for cooking)

Directions:

1. In a skillet, add some butter over medium heat.

2. In a bowl, add the eggs, salt, white pepper, and milk, then whisk well.

3. When the butter is hot, pour the egg mixture into it.

4. Cook the eggs until they are just set.

5. Sprinkle the cheese over the omelet.

6. Use a spatula to lift one side of the omelet, then fold it over. Continue cooking until the eggs have set.

7. Transfer the omelet to a plate and serve immediately.

Ham and Cheese

Ham and cheese is a classic combination that you would usually see on pizzas. This combination also works well on omelets as the two ingredients are tasty together!

Time: *15 minutes*

Serving Size: *2 servings*

Prep Time: *5 minutes*

Cook Time: *10 minutes*

Ingredients:

- 1 tbsp cream

- 1/3 cup of Colby cheese (shredded)

- 1/3 cup of ham (cooked, chopped)

- 3 eggs

- salt

- butter (for cooking)

Directions:

1. In a pan, add some butter over medium heat.

2. In a bowl, add the eggs, salt, and cream, then whisk to combine all of the ingredients well.

3. When the butter is hot, pour the egg mixture into it.

4. Cook the eggs until they are just set.

5. Sprinkle the chopped ham and cheese over the omelet.

6. Use a spatula to lift one side of the omelet, then fold it over. Continue cooking until the eggs have set.

7. Transfer the omelet to a plate and serve while hot.

Chapter 3:

Lunchbox Favorites

Lunchboxes are fun, delicious, and super versatile. It's also very easy to put different ingredients together to make colorful combinations that your child will surely enjoy. Here are some recipes to make with your little one to make sure they finish every bite!

DIY Sandwiches and Wraps

Cheesy Clubhouse

Clubhouse sandwiches are simple, tasty, and comforting. This has a twist to it as it contains more ingredients for your child to prepare with you.

Time: 25 *minutes*

Serving Size: 3 *servings*

Prep Time: 15 *minutes*

Cook Time: 10 *minutes*

Ingredients:

- 1 cup of cream cheese (softened)

- 1 tomato (sliced)

- 3 slices of smoked bacon (grilled, each slice cut in half)

- 1 carrot (peeled, grated)

- 9 cucumber slices

- 3 lettuce leaves

- 9 slices of bread (whole-wheat, toasted)

Directions:

1. In a bowl, add the carrot and cheese, then mix well.

2. Spread the cheesy carrot mixture over one side of 6 bread slices and over both sides of the other 2 slices of bread.

3. On 3 of the bread slices, add the sliced tomatoes and cucumber, then top with the bread slices that have cheesy carrot spread on both sides.

4. Add the bacon, then cover with another slice of bread.

5. Cut off the sandwich crusts and slice the sandwiches into small triangles.

6. Insert a toothpick into the middle of each small sandwich and serve.

Sweet and Savory

The great thing about wraps is that they are super easy and customizable. You can ask your child which ingredients they want and create different versions, such as these sweet and savory wrap varieties.

Time: 10 *minutes*

Serving Size: 1 *serving*

Prep Time: 10 *minutes*

Cook Time: *no cooking time*

Ingredients for the sweet wrap:

- 1 tbsp jelly

- 1 soft tortilla

- 1 tbsp peanut butter

Ingredients for the savory wrap:

- 1 soft tortilla

- 1 tbsp cream cheese

- 1/2 carrot (peeled, grated)

- 2 slices of ham

Directions:

1. Spread peanut butter all over one of the tortillas, then top with a layer of jelly.

2. Fold the sides of the tortilla to the middle, then roll it from the bottom to the top.

3. Use a knife to cut the tortilla in half, then place both halves on a plate.

4. Spread cream cheese all over the other tortilla.

5. Lay the ham slices on the tortilla, then top with grated carrot.

6. Fold the sides of the tortilla to the middle, then roll it from the bottom to the top.

7. Use a knife to cut the tortilla in half, then place both halves on a plate with the sweet wraps.

8. Serve immediately.

Grilled Cheese Pizza

Combining grilled cheese and pizza sounds like a wonderful dish, right? Although this recipe has more steps than the others, your efforts will surely pay off when you taste this delicious and unique sandwich.

Time: *15 minutes*

Serving Size: *2 servings*

Prep Time: *5 minutes*

Cook Time: *10 minutes*

Ingredients for the filling:

- 1/2 tsp chili sauce

- 1 1/2 tbsp sweet corn kernels

- 1 tbsp tomato sauce

- 1/8 cup of cheese (grated)

- 1/8 cup of mayonnaise

- 1/2 onion (finely chopped)

- 1/4 bell pepper (stem and seeds removed, finely chopped)

- 1/2 tomato (finely chopped)

- salt

- pepper

Ingredients for the sandwich:

- 1/4 tsp chili sauce

- 1/4 tsp mixed herbs (dried)

- 1 tbsp cheese (grated)

- 1 1/2 tbsp tomato sauce

- 2 slices of bread

- 2 slices of tomato

- 8 cucumber slices

- butter (for spreading)

Directions:

1. Add all the filling ingredients to a bowl and mix well.

2. Spread butter on one side of the bread slices, then top two slices of bread with the filling.

3. Add the other slice of bread on top with the buttered side facing the filling.

4. Spread tomato sauce over the top slices of bread, then add the pizza sandwich toppings.

5. Lightly toast the sandwiches in the toaster or by cooking them on the stove until the cheese melts.

6. Place the sandwiches on plates and slice them into triangles.

7. Serve while hot.

European Style

This lunch recipe is quick, simple, and super versatile. Serve this sandwich for lunch during your next picnic, and get ready to stun them all with its yummy taste.

Time: *10 minutes*

Serving Size: *2 servings*

Prep Time: *10 minutes*

Cook Time: *no cooking time*

Ingredients:

- 1 tsp lemon juice (freshly squeezed)
- 4 tbsp goat cheese (softened)
- 2 tsp fig jam
- 1/2 pear (cored, sliced)
- 2 soft tortillas (whole-wheat)
- 2 prosciutto slices

Directions:

1. Spread goat cheese all over the soft tortillas, then top with a layer of fig jam.
2. Top each tortilla with prosciutto slices.
3. In a bowl, add the sliced pears.
4. Drizzle with lemon juice, then toss to coat.
5. Add the sliced pears on top of the prosciutto.

6. Fold the sides of the tortillas to the middle, then roll them up from the bottom to the top.

7. Slice the tortillas in half and serve.

Egg Salad With Avocado

This egg salad sandwich elevates the classic with the addition of healthy ingredients. This is an excellent lunch special, and your child can even enjoy it as a snack!

Time: *10 minutes*

Serving Size: *2 servings*

Prep Time: *10 minutes*

Cook Time: *no cooking time*

Ingredients:

- 1 tbsp Greek yogurt (plain)

- 1/2 tsp yellow mustard

- 1 small avocado (peeled, pitted, sliced)

- 4 slices of bread

- 3 eggs (hard-boiled)

- a pinch of salt

- a pinch of pepper

Directions:

1. In a bowl, add the avocado slices and use a fork to mash until smooth.

2. Add the rest of the ingredients to the bowl except the eggs and bread, then mix well.

3. Add the eggs and use a fork to mash the eggs. Mix everything until well combined.

4. Spread the egg salad all over two of the bread slices, then top with another slice of bread.

5. Serve immediately.

Veggie Snack Packs

Basic Snack Pack

It's easy to make snack packs for your child that are filled with colorful veggies. Here is one example. Try to come up with your own combinations next time!

Time: *5 minutes*

Serving Size: *2 servings*

Prep Time: *5 minutes*

Cook Time: *no cooking time*

Ingredients:

- 1 cup of baby carrots (washed)

- 1/2 cup of ranch dressing (preferably homemade)

- 1 broccoli head (washed, cut into florets)

- 1 cup of grape tomatoes (washed)

Directions:

1. Add the ranch dressing in small plastic cups with lids, then place them in the middle of your child's lunch boxes.

2. Add the vegetables around the ranch dressing cups in airtight containers.

3. Cover the containers and place in the refrigerator until ready to serve.

Veggies and Beet Dip

Making your own dip at home is highly recommended, as you can use the freshest ingredients to make delicious combinations. Here is an example of a tasty veggie dip.

Time: 10 *minutes*

Serving Size: 2 *servings*

Prep Time: 10 *minutes*

Cook Time: *no cooking time*

Ingredients:

- 1/3 tsp sea salt

- 1/4 tsp cumin (ground)

- 1 tbsp extra virgin olive oil

- 1 tbsp water

- 1/8 cup of lemon juice (freshly squeezed)

- 1/8 cup of beet (cooked, peeled, diced)

- 1/8 cup of cup of tahini

- zest of 1/2 lemon

- 1 large clove of garlic (minced)

- 3/4 cup of chickpeas (cooked, drained, rinsed)

- tortilla chips, veggie sticks, or toast points (for serving)

Directions:

1. In a food processor, add the olive oil, tahini, garlic, lemon juice, lemon zest, cumin, salt, and water, then pulse until you get a smooth texture.

2. Add the beets and chickpeas, then continue to pulse for about 2 minutes until you get a very smooth texture.

3. Spoon the dip into a bowl and serve with tortilla chips, veggie sticks, or toast points.

Veggie Pizza Rolls

If you want your child to eat more veggies, you have to think of ways to present these healthy foods creatively. Here's a great idea for a nice lunch or snack option.

Time: *30 minutes*

Serving Size: *6 servings*

Prep Time: *8 minutes*

Cook Time: *22 minutes*

Ingredients:

- 1/4 cup of carrots (peeled, grated)

- 1/4 cup of bell pepper (seeds and stems removed, finely chopped)

- 1/2 cup of spinach (finely chopped)

- 3/4 cup of mozzarella cheese (shredded)

- 1/2 cup of tomato sauce

- 8-ounce pizza dough (homemade or store-bought)

- cooking spray

Directions:

1. Preheat your oven to 400°F and use cooking spray to lightly grease a muffin tin.

2. Add the pizza dough to a lightly floured surface, then use a rolling pin to roll the dough into a rectangle.

3. Spread the tomato sauce all over the dough, then top with carrot, spinach, and bell pepper.

4. Sprinkle the mozzarella cheese all over the other toppings.

5. Starting from the bottom, roll the pizza up tightly.

6. Use a knife to slice the pizza roll into 12 pieces, then place each piece in the muffin tin.

7. Place the muffin tin in the oven and bake the pizza rolls for about 20 to 22 minutes.

8. After baking, take the muffin tin out and allow the pizza rolls to cool down slightly.

9. Transfer the pizza rolls to a plate and serve.

Corn and Zucchini Fritters With Fruits

These savory fritters are crispy and tasty and made with healthy ingredients. Add them to your child's lunch box along with other foods for a filling meal.

Time: *15 minutes*

Serving Size: *6 servings*

Prep Time: *5 minutes*

Cook Time: *10 minutes*

Ingredients:

- 1/8 tsp salt

- 1/8 tsp onion powder

- 1/8 cup of milk

- 1/4 cup of cheddar cheese (grated)

- 1/2 tsp baking powder

- 1/4 cup of flour (whole wheat)

- 1/2 cup of zucchini (grated)

- 1/2 cup of corn kernels (fresh)

- 1 egg

- fruits (your child's favorite, sliced)

- olive oil (for cooking)

Directions:

1. Place the zucchini on a cheesecloth, then gather the edges to wrap the grated vegetable.

2. Squeeze the moisture out of the zucchini, then place it in a bowl.

3. Add the rest of the ingredients except the oil and fruits, then mix well.

4. In a skillet, add some olive oil over medium heat.

5. When the oil is hot, add heaping tablespoons of fritter batter to the skillet, making sure not to add too many pieces.

6. Cook each side for about 2 to 3 minutes, then transfer the fritters to a plate lined with paper towels to drain the excess oil.

7. When the fritters have cooled down, serve them for lunch along with your child's favorite sliced fruits.

Lentil Quesadillas

Lentils are a type of legume that is very nutritious. Adding lentils to any dish will make them more filling and a lot healthier too.

Time: *25 minutes*

Serving Size: *3 servings*

Prep Time: *10 minutes*

Cook Time: *15 minutes*

Ingredients:

- 1/4 cup of salsa (homemade or store-bought)

- 1/4 cup of carrot (peeled, grated)

- 1/2 cup of lentils (cooked, drained)

- 1/4 cup of spinach (finely chopped)

- 3/4 cup of cheddar cheese (grated)

- 3 soft tortillas

Directions:

1. In a bowl, add all of the ingredients except the tortillas, then mix everything well.

2. In a skillet, add a soft tortilla over medium-high heat.

3. When the tortilla is warm, flip it over and add 1/3 of the filling to one side, then take the other side and fold it over.

4. Heat the quesadilla for about 2 to 3 minutes using the back of a spatula to press down and squish everything together.

5. Flip the quesadilla over and continue cooking for about 2 to 3 minutes.

6. Transfer the quesadilla to a plate and repeat the cooking steps for the other 2 tortillas.

7. Slice the quesadillas into triangles and allow them to cool down slightly before serving.

Homemade Lunchbox Treats

Pasta Salad

Have you ever tried giving your child pasta salad? This dish is delicious, simple, and super customizable, which means your little one can add any ingredient they want to it!

Time: *25 minutes*

Serving Size: *2 servings*

Prep Time: *14 minutes*

Cook Time: *11 minutes*

Ingredients:

- 1/2 tbsp mayonnaise

- 1 tbsp Greek yogurt (plain)

- 1 tbsp lemon juice (freshly squeezed)

- 3 tbsp pesto (fresh)

- 1/4 cup of cherry tomatoes (cut into quarters)

- 1/2 cup of chicken (cooked; you can also use cooked prawns, ham, hard-boiled egg slices, and more)

- 1/2 cup of mixed veggies like green beans, peas, sliced cucumbers (cooked)

- 1 cup of pasta (uncooked)

- water (for cooking the pasta)

Directions:

1. Fill a pot with water, place it over medium heat, and bring to a boil.

2. When the water is boiling, add the pasta. Cook for about 11 minutes, depending on what's written on the package instructions.

3. After cooking the pasta, drain the water.

4. Add the pesto to the pasta, mix well, and set aside to cool down.

5. When the pasta has cooled down, add the yogurt, mayonnaise, lemon juice, tomatoes, and mixed veggies, then toss to combine.

6. Spoon the pasta salad into your child's lunchbox and top with chicken.

7. Pack up your child's lunchbox for school!

Savory Potato Cakes

Potato cakes are very appealing to kids because they are crunchy on the outside and soft on the inside. If you have some leftover mashed potato, you can easily make this dish!

Time: *25 minutes*

Serving Size: *2 servings*

Prep Time: *5 minutes*

Cook Time: *20 minutes*

Ingredients:

- 1/8 cup of all-purpose flour
- 1/4 cup of peas (frozen, thawed)
- 1/2 cup of cheese (grated)
- 1 cup of mashed potato (leftover or freshly made)
- 1/2 shallot (finely chopped)
- 1 slice of bacon (diced)
- cooking spray

Directions:

1. In a pan, add the diced bacon over medium-high heat.

2. Cook the bacon for about 2 to 3 minutes, then transfer to a plate lined with a paper towel to drain the excess oil.

3. After draining the oil, add the bacon to a bowl along with the rest of the ingredients except the flour and cooking spray. Mix well.

4. Use your hands to take portions of the mixture and form each portion into a small ball.

5. Roll the balls in the flour to coat them lightly.

6. Use cooking spray to grease a pan and place it over medium heat.

7. When the oil is hot, add the potato balls, then use a spatula to flatten them slightly.

8. Cook each side for about 8 minutes until golden brown on the outside.

9. Transfer the cooked potato cakes to a plate lined with a paper towel to drain the excess oil.

10. Allow the potato cakes to cool down slightly before packing them in your child's lunchbox.

Fish Finger Sandwiches

Children are really fond of fish fingers, whether they're homemade or bought from the supermarket ready-to-cook. Add these crunchy fish fingers to sandwiches for a tasty lunchtime treat.

Time: *25 minutes*

Serving Size: *2 servings*

Prep Time: *15 minutes*

Cook Time: *10 minutes*

Ingredients:

- 2 tbsp mayonnaise (for serving)

- 1 1/2 tbsp all-purpose flour

- 1/4 cup of iceberg lettuce (shredded)

- 1/4 cup of breadcrumbs

- 1 cod or pollock fillet (cut into 4 thick slices)

- 2 brioche hot dog buns

- 1 egg (beaten)

- salt

- pepper

- sunflower oil (for cooking)

Directions:

1. Add the flour, salt, pepper, and m in a shallow dish. Mix well.

2. In a second bowl, add the beaten egg.

3. In a third bowl, add the breadcrumbs.

4. Coat one of the fish slices in seasoned flour, dip in the egg, coat with breadcrumbs, and place on a plate.

5. Repeat the coating steps for the rest of the fish slices.

6. Add some sunflower oil to a pan over medium-high heat, then swirl the pan around to coat it with oil.

7. When the oil is hot enough, add the fish fingers. Cook each side for about 3 to 5 minutes.

8. After cooking, transfer the fish fingers to a plate lined with a paper towel, then sprinkle with some salt.

9. Lightly toast the brioche hotdog buns, then spread mayonnaise all over the insides.

10. Add 2 fish fingers in each bun, then top with shredded lettuce.

11. Pack the sandwiches in your child's lunchboxes for school.

Mini Quiches

These mini quiches are tasty, easy to make, and they make for a very fancy lunch option for your child. Making them is a lot of fun too since you can allow your child to choose their favorite fillings for the quiches.

Time: *45 minutes*

Serving Size: *3 servings*

Prep Time: *20 minutes*

Cook Time: *25 minutes*

Ingredients:

- 1/8 cup of basil (fresh, finely shredded)

- 1/8 cup of goat's cheese (crumbled)

- 1/4 cup of cream

- 2 sheets of ready-rolled shortcrust pastry (thawed)

- 3 eggs (lightly beaten)

- 3 slices of salami (thinly sliced)

- cooking spray

- pepper

- salt

Directions:

1. Preheat your oven to 390°F and use cooking spray to grease a mini muffin tin lightly.

2. Use a round cookie cutter to cut out 12 circles from the ready-rolled shortcrust pastry.

3. Line the muffin tin with the pastry circles, then use your finger to press down. Use a fork to prick some holes on the bottom of the pastry circles.

4. Place the muffin tin in the oven and bake the quiche crusts for about 10 minutes.

5. After baking, take the muffin tin out of the oven.

6. In a small jug, add the cream, eggs, salt, and pepper, then whisk well.

7. Sprinkle salami and basil into the quiche crusts, pour some of the cream mixture into each crust, and top with cheese.

8. Place the muffin tin in the oven and bake the mini quiches for about 13 to 15 minutes.

9. After baking, take the muffin tin out of the oven.

10. Allow the mini quiches to cool down slightly before packing them in your child's lunchbox.

Cottage Pie Cakes With Dip

This tasty lunchtime option is perfect for children as it contains a lot of healthy ingredients. It's affordable and easy to make too. Perfect!

Time: 30 *minutes (chilling time not included)*

Serving Size: 2 *servings*

Prep Time: 15 *minutes*

Cook Time: 15 *minutes*

Ingredients:

- 3 tsp extra virgin olive oil (divided)

- 2 tsp tomato paste

- 2 tbsp water (cold)

- 1 tbsp parsley (fresh, chopped)

- 1/4 cup of all-purpose flour

- 3/4 cup of mashed potato (chilled)

- 1/4 cup of peas (frozen, thawed)

- 1/3 lb beef mince

- 1 shallot (thinly sliced)

- cherry tomatoes (cut in half for serving)

- 1/2 small carrot (peeled, grated)

- salad leaves (for serving)

Directions:

1. In a saucepan, add 1 teaspoon of olive oil over medium-high heat.

2. When the oil is hot, add the carrot and shallot. Cook for about 2 minutes.

3. Add the beef mince and cook for about 5 minutes while using your spatula to break up the clumps of meat.

4. Add the water and tomato paste, then continue cooking for about 1 minute.

5. Add the peas and continue cooking for about 1 minute.

6. Transfer the mixture to a bowl and allow to cool down for about 5 minutes.

7. After cooling, add the flour, parsley, and mashed potato, then mix to combine.

8. Use your hands to take portions of the mixture and form each portion into a patty.

9. Place the patties on a baking tray, then place in the refrigerator to chill for about 15 minutes.

10. After chilling, take the baking tray out of the oven.

11. In a frying pan, add the rest of the olive oil over medium-high heat.

12. When the oil is hot enough, add the patties. Cook each side for about 2 to 3 minutes.

13. Transfer the cottage pie cakes to a plate lined with a paper towel to drain any excess oil, then allow them to cool down.

14. Add the cottage pie cakes to your child's lunchbox along with some salad greens and cherry tomatoes.

Chapter 4:

Snack Time Fun

Children love snacks! They can have snacks in the morning and the afternoon. Sometimes, they can even enjoy a midnight snack. No matter what time of the day it is, inviting your child to prepare snacks with you will surely make them feel even more joyful about this meal of the day.

Trail Mix Extravaganza

Cookies and Candies

Kids love cookies and candies! Prepare these fun ingredients and ask your child to scoop their own portion of trail mix to bring to school or even to your next picnic.

Time: 5 *minutes*

Serving Size: 8 *servings*

Prep Time: 5 *minutes*

Cook Time: *no cooking time*

Ingredients:

- 1/2 cup of cashews

- 1/2 cup of Cheerios toasted oat cereal (any flavor)

- 1/2 cup of cranberries (dried)

- 1/2 cup of goldfish crackers

- 1/2 cup of miniature M&M's

- 1/2 cup miniature pretzel twists

- 1/2 cup of peanut butter chips

Directions:

1. Prepare all of the ingredients in small containers and lay them out on a table.

2. Prepare 8 small containers and ask your child to scoop the ingredients into each of them.

3. Cover the containers and pack them up!

Nuts and Sweets

Nuts are a healthy and filling snack option as they contain essential nutrients. Mix them up with sweets for a tasty treat your child will enjoy.

Time: *5 minutes*

Serving Size: *8 servings*

Prep Time: *5 minutes*

Cook Time: *no cooking time*

Ingredients:

- 1/2 cup of M&M's

- 1/2 cup of walnuts

- 1 cup of almonds (roasted)

- 1 cup of peanuts (lightly salted)

- 1 cup of raisins

Directions:

1. Place all of the ingredients in small bowls and lay them out on a table.

2. Prepare 8 small containers and ask your child to scoop the ingredients into each of them.

3. Cover the containers and serve!

Fruits and Cereals

Mixing cereals and fruits is a fun and tasty way for your child to enjoy snack time more. The great thing about this combination is that there are countless options to choose from.

Time: 5 *minutes*

Serving Size: 4 *servings*

Prep Time: *5 minutes*

Cook Time: *no cooking time*

Ingredients:

- 1/2 cup of your child's favorite dried fruit

- 1/2 cup of your child's favorite fruit chips

- 1/2 cup of your child's favorite vegetable chips

- 1/2 cup of cashews

- 1/2 cup of coconut chips

- 1/2 cup of walnut halves (lightly salted)

- 2 cups of your child's favorite cereal

Directions:

1. Add all of the ingredients in individual containers and lay them out on a table.

2. Prepare 4 small containers with lids and ask your child to scoop the ingredients into each of them.

3. Cover the containers and pack them up!

6Tiny Treats and Sweets

Most trail mixes have something sweet in them to provide an energy boost to your little one. Here is another healthy mix of treats for you and your child to enjoy.

Time: *5 minutes*

Serving Size: *8 servings*

Prep Time: *5 minutes*

Cook Time: *no cooking time*

Ingredients:

- 1/2 cup of sunflower seeds

- 1/4 cup of dark chocolate chips

- 1 cup of raisins

- 1 cup of cashews

- 1 1/2 cups of almonds (roasted, lightly salted)

Directions:

1. Add all of the ingredients to a bowl and toss to combine.

2. Prepare 8 small containers and ask your child to scoop the mixed ingredients into each of them.

3. Cover the containers and serve!

Nut-Free Treats

If your child is allergic to nuts, you don't have to add them to your trail mix. As you may know by now, trail mix can contain anything you want! So here's a nut-free recipe for you to try out.

Time: *10 minutes*

Serving Size: *8 servings*

Prep Time: *5 minutes*

Cook Time: *5 minutes*

Ingredients:

- 1 tbsp brown sugar

- 1 tsp cinnamon

- 2 tbsp butter (melted)

- 1/2 cup of chocolate-covered sunflower seeds

- 1/2 cup of blueberries (dried)

- 3/4 cup of sunflower seeds

- 2 cups of rice crackers

- 2 cups of Cheerios cereal

Directions:

1. In a microwave-safe bowl, add the pumpkin seeds and cereal, then toss to combine.

2. Drizzle the butter into the bowl and toss again.

3. Sprinkle brown sugar and cinnamon into the bowl and toss to coat.

4. Place the bowl in the microwave and heat it up for about 90 seconds.

5. Take the bowl out and mix everything together.

6. Place the bowl back in the microwave and heat for another 90 seconds.

7. Take the bowl out and pour the mixture onto a baking sheet for the mixture to cool down.

8. When the mixture has cooled down, add the rest of the ingredients and mix well.

9. Prepare 8 small containers and ask your child to scoop the mixed ingredients into each of them.

10. Cover the containers and pack them up!

Yogurt Parfait Pops

Breakfast Pops

Parfaits are fun, colorful, and they can be very nutritious depending on the ingredients you use to make them. Here is an example of a yogurt breakfast pop for your child.

Time: *15 minutes (freezing time not included)*

Serving Size: *6 servings*

Prep Time: *15 minutes*

Cook Time: *no cooking time*

Ingredients:

- 2 1/2 cups of yogurt (fat-free, vanilla flavor)

- 1 cup of granola

- 1/2 cup of blueberries (fresh)

Directions:

1. Spoon some yogurt into popsicle molds, then top with a layer of granola, and a layer of blueberries.

2. Continue to add layers of yogurt, granola, and fruit until you've used up all of the ingredients.

3. Place the popsicle mold in the freezer and freeze for a minimum of 6 hours.

4. Serve frozen.

Blueberry Chia

Blueberries are one of the healthiest fruits out there, which makes them an excellent addition to your child's diet. Make your child feel excited about eating fruits by making these parfait pops with them.

Time: *5 minutes (freezing time not included)*

Serving Size: *6 servings*

Prep Time: *5 minutes*

Cook Time: *no cooking time*

Ingredients:

- 1 tbsp honey

- 1 tsp chia seeds

- 1/8 cup of milk

- 3/4 cup of Greek yogurt (plain)

- 3/4 cup of blueberries (fresh)

Directions:

1. In a bowl, add the milk, yogurt, honey, and chia seeds, then mix well.

2. Spoon the yogurt mixture into popsicle molds, then top with a layer of blueberries.

3. Continue to add layers of yogurt and granola until you've used everything up.

4. Place the popsicle mold in the freezer and freeze for a minimum of 4 hours.

5. Serve frozen.

Fruity Granola

Adding different types of fruits to your child's parfait pops will make them healthier and tastier. Here is an easy and fruity recipe to make with your little one now.

Time: *5 minutes (freezing time not included)*

Serving Size: *6 servings*

Prep Time: *5 minutes*

Cook Time: *no cooking time*

Ingredients:

- 1/4 cup of your child's favorite breakfast cereal

- 1/2 cup of mixed fruit (fresh, finely chopped)

- 6 small yogurt cups (fruit-flavored)

Directions:

1. Transfer the yogurt from the fruit cups to a bowl.

2. Spoon the yogurt back into the yogurt cups, then top with a layer of cereal and a layer of mixed fruits.

3. Continue to add layers of yogurt, cereal, and fruits until you've used up all of the ingredients.

4. Place the yogurt cups in the freezer and freeze for a minimum of 4 hours.

5. Serve frozen.

Rainbow Fruits

You may have heard how it's a good idea to "eat the rainbow." This usually refers to adding vegetables of all colors to your plate. This time, you can get your child to eat the rainbow by adding fruits of different colors to a parfait pop.

Time: *5 minutes (freezing time not included)*

Serving Size: *6 servings*

Prep Time: *5 minutes*

Cook Time: *no cooking time*

Ingredients:

- 1/8 cup of raspberries (fresh)

- 1/8 cup of melon (finely chopped)

- 1/8 cup of mango (finely chopped)

- 1/8 cup of honeydew (finely chopped)

- 1/8 cup of blueberries (finely chopped)

- 1/8 cup of grapes (seedless, finely chopped)

- 1 1/2 cups of Greek yogurt (plain)

Directions:

1. In a bowl, add the fruits and mix well.

2. Spoon the yogurt into popsicle molds, then top with a layer of mixed fruits.

3. Continue to add layers of yogurt and fruits until you've used up all of the ingredients.

4. Place the popsicle mold in the freezer and freeze for a minimum of 4 hours.

5. Serve frozen.

Very Berry

Berries are delicious, healthy, and super versatile. Here's a recipe for parfait pops with fresh berries that will make your child smile with every bite.

Time: *5 minutes*

Serving Size: *6 servings*

Prep Time: *5 minutes*

Cook Time: *no cooking time*

Ingredients:

- 1 tsp vanilla extract

- 3 tbsp honey

- 1/4 cup of milk

- 2/3 cup of granola

- 1 1/2 cups of Greek yogurt (plain)

- 3 cups of mixed berries like strawberries, raspberries, and blueberries (fresh or frozen, roughly chopped)

Directions:

1. In a saucepan, add the fruit and half of the honey over medium-high heat.

2. Gently stir while heating up the fruits and bring to a gentle simmer.

3. Continue simmering for about 8 to 10 minutes until the berries turn into a chunky jam.

4. Take the saucepan off the heat, add the vanilla extract, and mix well.

5. Allow the berry jam to cool down to room temperature.

6. When the berry jam has cooled down, prepare the yogurt. Add the yogurt to a bowl along with the milk, and the rest of the honey. Mix well.

7. Spoon the yogurt mixture into popsicle molds, then top with a layer of berry jam and a layer of granola.

8. Continue to add layers of yogurt, berry jam, and granola until you've used everything up.

9. Place the popsicle mold in the freezer and freeze for a minimum of 6 hours.

10. Serve frozen.

Crunchy Veggie Chips

Rainbow Veggies

Eating veggies can be a lot of fun for kids, especially when you prepare them in different ways. Here is a recipe for crunchy veggie chips that your child will surely love.

Time: 15 *minutes*

Serving Size: 2 *servings*

Prep Time: 5 *minutes*

Cook Time: 10 *minutes*

Ingredients:

- 1/2 tsp olive oil

- 1/2 tsp pepper

- 1/2 tsp salt

- 1 carrot (peeled, sliced into strips)

- 1 beet (peeled, sliced into strips)

- 1 golden beet (peeled, sliced into strips)

- 1 turnip (peeled, sliced into strips)

- 1 sweet potato (peeled, sliced into strips)

- 1 zucchini (peeled, sliced into strips)

Directions:

1. Preheat your oven to 400°F and use a sheet of parchment paper to line a baking sheet.

2. In a bowl, add all of the vegetables.

3. Season with salt and pepper, then drizzle the olive oil all over the veggies.

4. Toss to coat and season the veggies.

5. Transfer the veggies to a baking sheet, then spread them all out in an even layer making sure that none of them are overlapping with each other.

6. Place the baking sheet in the oven and bake the veggies for about 20 minutes. Halfway through the cooking time, take the baking sheet out of the oven and flip the veggies over to cook them evenly.

7. After baking, take the baking sheet out of the oven.

8. Allow the veggie chips to cool down slightly before serving.

Zesty Zucchini

This is a quick and simple recipe that will encourage your child to eat more veggies. It's fun to make and even more fun to enjoy together.

Time: *1 hour (or more), 10 minutes*

Serving Size: *4 servings*

Prep Time: *10 minutes*

Cook Time: *1 hour (or more)*

Ingredients:

- 4 zucchinis (peeled, sliced thinly)

- pepper

- salt

- oil

Directions:

1. Preheat your oven on low, and use parchment paper to line baking sheets.

2. In a bowl, add the zucchini, then season with salt and pepper. Toss to season the veggies.

3. Add the seasoned zucchini chips to the baking sheet in a single layer.

4. Place the baking sheet in the oven and bake the zucchini chips for about 1 hour or more. Check the chips every half hour until they are cooked.

5. After baking, take the baking sheet out of the oven.

6. Allow the zucchini chips to cool down completely before serving.

Chip Fries

These homemade chip fries are easy, quick, and super tasty. Whip up a combination of different vegetables for a colorful, crispy, and nutritious treat!

Time: *30 minutes*

Serving Size: *4 servings*

Prep Time: *10 minutes*

Cook Time: *20 minutes*

Ingredients:

- 2 parsnips (peeled, sliced into strips, tossed with 1 tbsp oil, 1 tbsp fresh thyme, and the zest of 1/2 lemon)

- 2 potatoes (peeled, sliced into strips, tossed with 1 tbsp oil, 1/2 tbsp paprika, and 1/2 tsp fresh thyme)

- 2 sweet potatoes (peeled, sliced into strips, tossed with 1 tbsp oil and 1 tsp sumac)

- 2 zucchinis (peeled, sliced into strips, tossed with 1 tbsp oil, 1 tbsp polenta, and 1/2 tbsp grated Parmesan)

- 4 carrots (peeled, sliced into strips, tossed with 1 tbsp oil and 1/2 tbsp cumin seeds)

Directions:

1. Preheat your oven to 400°F and use a sheet of parchment paper to line a baking sheet.

2. Toss the vegetable chip fries in separate bowls with their own spices and spice blends.

3. Add the vegetable chip fries to a baking sheet and arrange them in a single layer.

4. Place the baking sheet in the oven and bake the vegetable chip fries for about 20 minutes. Halfway through the cooking time, take the baking sheet out of the oven and shake the baking sheet to cook the vegetable chip fries evenly.

5. After baking, take the baking sheet out of the oven.

6. Allow the vegetable chip fries to cool down before serving.

Cheesy Sweet Potato Curls

These sweet potato curls are crispy and wonderfully cheesy. If you don't have a spiralizer, you can just cut them up into fries before cooking.

Time: *35 minutes*

Serving Size: *2 servings*

Prep Time: *15 minutes*

Cook Time: *20 minutes*

Ingredients:

- 1/8 tsp salt

- 1/8 tsp pepper

- 1/3 tsp garlic powder

- 1/8 cup of Parmesan cheese (finely grated)

- 1 tbsp extra-virgin olive oil (divided)

- 1 large sweet potato (peeled, spiralized)

Directions:

1. Preheat your oven to 425°F and place a baking sheet inside to heat it up.

2. In a bowl, add the spiralized sweet potato, garlic powder, pepper, salt, and half of the oil, then toss to combine.

3. Take the baking sheet out of the oven and line it with a sheet of parchment paper.

4. Add the sweet potato curls to the baking sheet and arrange them in a single layer.

5. Place the baking sheet in the oven and bake the sweet potato curls for about 15 minutes.

6. After baking, take the baking sheet out of the oven.

7. Transfer the sweet potato curls to a bowl along with the Parmesan cheese and the rest of the oil, then toss to combine.

8. Transfer the sweet potato curls back to the baking sheet.

9. Place the baking sheet back in the oven and bake the potato curls for about 5 minutes more.

10. After baking, take the baking sheet out of the oven.

11. Transfer the sweet potato curls to a bowl and allow them to cool down.

12. Serve.

Crispy Kale

Kale has become a very popular vegetable because it is so healthy and versatile. Include this superfood in your child's diet by transforming it into tasty and crispy chips.

Time: *20 minutes*

Serving Size: *2 servings*

Prep Time: *8 minutes*

Cook Time: *12 minutes*

Ingredients:

- 1/2 tbsp extra-virgin olive oil

- 1 small bunch of kale (tough stems removed, torn into bite-sized pieces)

- a pinch of salt

Directions:

1. Preheat your oven to 400°F and use a sheet of parchment paper to line a baking sheet.

2. In a bowl, add the kale leaves, olive oil, and a pinch of salt, then toss to coat the leaves.

3. Transfer the kale leaves to a baking sheet, then spread them out in a single layer.

4. Place the baking sheet in the oven and bake the kale leaves for about 8 to 12 minutes. Halfway through the cooking time, take the baking sheet out and shake it around to bake the kale chips evenly.

5. After baking, take the baking sheet out of the oven.

6. Transfer the kale chips to a bowl and allow them to cool down.

7. Serve.

Chapter 5:

Creative Dinner Ideas

For many families, dinner is the meal that they all get to share together. Whether this is true for your family or not, asking your child to help you prepare dinner will be a wonderful bonding experience. You can whip up simple, delicious, and creative meals for everyone to enjoy together!

Build-Your-Own Pizza Night

Tiny Pizzas for Tiny Kids

Kids really enjoy eating pizza, especially if it contains their favorite toppings. Give your child a treat by making these tiny pizzas together!

Time: *30 minutes*

Serving Size: *4 servings*

Prep Time: *12 minutes*

Cook Time: *18 minutes*

Ingredients for the pizza crust:

- 1/2 tsp sugar (granulated)

- 1/2 tsp salt

- 1/2 tbsp olive oil

- 1/2 cup of water (warm)

- 1 1/8 tsp dry active yeast

- 1 1/8cups of all-purpose flour

Ingredients for the pizza toppings:

- cheese (shredded)

- pizza sauce (jarred)

- your child's favorite toppings, such as pepperoni slices, sausage slices, olives, mushrooms, and more

Directions:

1. Preheat your oven to 425°F and use a sheet of parchment paper to line a baking sheet.

2. In a bowl, add the warm water, yeast, and sugar, then mix well.

3. Let sit for about 10 minutes until you see small bubbles form on the surface.

4. Add the flour to the bowl and mix well until you form a dough.

5. Place the dough on a clean, floured surface and knead for about 1 to 2 minutes until the dough becomes elastic and smooth.

6. Roll the dough into a ball and coat it with oil.

7. Place the dough ball into a bowl and cover with a sheet of cling wrap.

8. Let sit for about 5 minutes.

9. Take the dough ball out of the bowl and divide it into 4. Roll each portion into a ball, then use a rolling pin to flatten it to form a small pizza crust. Do the same for the other 3 dough balls.

10. Spread pizza sauce all over the small pizza crusts, then sprinkle cheese over the sauce.

11. Top with different toppings.

12. Place the small pizzas on the baking sheet, making sure the crusts don't overlap.

13. Place the baking sheet in the oven. Bake the small pizzas for about 15 to 18 minutes.

14. After baking, take the baking sheet out of the oven, and allow the small pizzas to cool down slightly.

15. Slice and serve while warm.

Rainbow Veggies

Encourage your child to eat more veggies by adding them to pizza. Use veggies with different colors for a treat for the eyes and the taste buds.

Time: 40 *minutes*

Serving Size: 2 *servings*

Prep Time: 20 *minutes*

Cook Time: 20 *minutes*

Ingredients:

- 1 tbsp pesto (fresh)

- 2 tbsp tomato purée

- 1/8 cup of broccoli florets (finely sliced)

- 2/3 cup of small mozzarella cheese balls

- 1 2/3 cups of mixed yellow and red tomatoes (sliced)

- 1 pizza crust (frozen, thawed, you can also make your own pizza dough)

- 4 green olives (pitted, sliced)

- a handful of basil leaves (fresh, for serving)

Directions:

1. Preheat your oven to 350°F and use a sheet of parchment to line a baking sheet.

2. Place the pizza dough on the baking sheet and spread tomato purée all over it.

3. Add the pizza toppings all around, then drizzle with fresh pesto.

4. Place the baking sheet in the oven. Bake the pizza for about 15 to 20 minutes.

5. After baking, take the baking sheet out of the oven and sprinkle fresh basil leaves all over.

6. Slice and serve while warm.

Pizza on Toast

Have you ever tried making pizza on a piece of toast? This is a fun way to prepare single servings of pizza for your child and the rest of the family.

Time: *25 minutes*

Serving Size: *3 servings*

Prep Time: *10 minutes*

Cook Time: *15 minutes*

Ingredients:

- 1/4 cup of mini pepperoni slices

- 1 cup of mozzarella cheese (shredded)

- 1/2 cup of pizza sauce

- 1/2 tbsp parsley (fresh, chopped)

- 3 slices of bread

Directions:

1. Preheat your oven to 350°F and use a sheet of parchment paper to line a baking sheet.

2. Place the slices of bread on the baking sheet and spread pizza sauce all over them.

3. Top each slice with mozzarella cheese and mini pepperoni slices.

4. Place the baking sheet in the oven. Bake the pizza toasts for about 13 to 15 minutes.

5. After baking, take the baking sheet out of the oven, and sprinkle parsley leaves all over the pizza roast slices.

6. Serve while warm.

Mac & Cheese on Top

Have you ever tried combining pizza with mac & cheese? This is a very indulgent pizza treat that your child will surely enjoy making and eating with you.

Time: *35 minutes*

Serving Size: *4 servings*

Prep Time: *15 minutes*

Cook Time: *20 minutes*

Ingredients:

- 1/4 tsp Italian seasoning

- 1/4 tsp garlic powder

- 1 cup of mozzarella cheese (shredded, divided)

- 1 cup of cheddar cheese (shredded, divided)

- 1 box of macaroni and cheese

- olive oil (for brushing)

- black pepper

- kosher salt

- 1 large pizza crust (frozen, thawed)

- parsley (freshly chopped)

Directions:

1. Preheat your oven to 450°F and use a sheet of parchment paper to line a large baking sheet.

2. Cook the macaroni and cheese according to the instructions on the box.

3. After cooking, add half of the cheddar and half of the mozzarella cheese to the pot and mix until the cheese melts and everything is well combined.

4. Brush olive oil all over the surface of the pizza crust, then top with garlic powder.

5. Place the pizza crust on the baking sheet.

6. Place the baking sheet in the oven. Bake the pizza crust for about 10 minutes.

7. After baking, take the baking sheet out of the oven.

8. Spoon the macaroni and cheese onto the pizza crust and spread it all over.

9. Sprinkle the rest of the cheddar cheese and mozzarella cheese all over the pizza.

10. Place the baking sheet back in the oven. Bake the pizza for about 10 minutes more.

11. After baking, take the baking sheet out of the oven and sprinkle fresh parsley leaves all over the pizza.

12. Slice and serve while warm.

Build Your Own

Make pizza night fun for the whole family by creating this easy build-your-own pizza dish. The only thing you need to do is prepare the ingredients and serve!

Time: *20 minutes*

Serving Size: *4 servings*

Prep Time: *10 minutes*

Cook Time: *10 minutes*

Ingredients:

- 1/8 cup of olives (pitted, sliced)

- 1/8 cup of onions

- 1 cup of pepperoni slices

- 2 cups of pasta sauce

- 2 cups of mozzarella cheese (shredded)

- 4 slices of flatbread

Directions:

1. Preheat your oven to 450°F and use a sheet of parchment paper to line a large baking sheet.

2. Prepare all of the ingredients on the table.

3. Spread pizza sauce all over the flatbread slices.

4. Sprinkle cheese all over the flatbread slices, then add your favorite toppings.

5. Place the flatbread pizzas on a baking sheet.

6. Place the baking sheet in the oven. Bake the flatbread pizzas for about 8 to 10 minutes.

7. After baking, take the baking sheet out of the oven.

8. Serve the flatbread pizzas while warm.

Pasta Party With Homemade Sauce

Classic Meatball Pasta

Children love pasta and when it comes to this dish, meatball pasta is the most popular. Teach your child how to make this classic dish, then share it with everyone!

Time: *45 minutes*

Serving Size: *3 servings*

Prep Time: *15 minutes*

Cook Time: *30 minutes*

Ingredients for the meatballs:

- 1/2 tbsp olive oil

- 1/2 tbsp oregano (dried)

- 1/4 cup of parmesan cheese (finely grated)

- 1/2 lb lean beef mince

- 1/2 small onion (coarsely grated)

- 1 egg

- 1 small carrot (peeled, finely grated)

- 4 large sausages

Ingredients for the sauce:

- 1/2 tbsp olive oil

- 1/2 tbsp tomato purée

- 1 cup of tomato (canned, chopped)

- 1 small cucumber (peeled, coarsely grated)

- 2 cloves of garlic (finely grated)

- a pinch of caster sugar

- a splash of red wine vinegar

- spaghetti (cooked, for serving)

Directions:

1. Slice off one end of the sausages, then squeeze the meat out into a bowl.

2. Add the beef mince to the bowl along with the rest of the meatball ingredients, except for the olive oil. Mix well.

3. Use your hands to take portions of the mixture. Roll each portion into a bowl and place on a plate.

4. In a saucepan, add the olive oil over medium heat.

5. When the oil is hot, add the meatballs. Cook the meatballs until all of the sides are browned.

6. Transfer the half-cooked meatballs back to the plate and set aside.

7. In a saucepan, add the olive oil over medium heat.

8. When the oil is hot, add the garlic and cucumber. Cook for about 5 minutes until mushy and soft.

9. Add the vinegar, sugar, and tomato puree. Cook for about 1 minute.

10. Add the tomatoes, mix well, and allow to simmer for about 5 minutes.

11. Add the meatballs to the saucepan and allow to simmer for about 15 minutes while stirring gently.

12. Pour the sauce and meatballs over cooked spaghetti noodles.

13. Serve while hot.

Bacon Cheeseburger

Cheeseburgers are yummy, comforting, and fun to make. Make the classic burger into sauce for your pasta to excite your child with every bite!

Time: 30 *minutes*

Serving Size: 3 *servings*

Prep Time: 5 *minutes*

Cook Time: 25 *minutes*

Ingredients:

- 1/4 cup of water

- 1/2 cup of penne pasta (uncooked)

- 1/2 cup of cheddar cheese (shredded)

- 1/2 lb ground beef

- 2/3 cup of condensed tomato soup (canned, undiluted)

- 3 strips of bacon (uncooked, diced)

- water (for cooking the pasta)

Directions:

1. Fill a pot with water and place it over medium heat. Bring to a boil.

2. When the water is boiling, add the pasta. Cook according to the directions on the package.

3. After cooking, drain the water and place the cooked pasta in a bowl. Set aside.

4. In a skillet, add the bacon. Cook for about 4 to 5 minutes until crispy.

5. Use a slotted spoon to scoop the cooked bacon out of the skillet and place it on a plate lined with a paper towel.

6. Drain the oil and add the pasta to the skillet.

7. Add the water, beef, bacon, and soup, then mix well. Cook for about 2 to 3 minutes until heated through.

8. Scoop the cooked pasta with sauce into bowls and top with cheese.

9. Serve while hot.

Roasted Veggies

A fun way to add more veggies to your child's diet is by adding it to pasta sauce, such as in this recipe. Roasting the veggies before adding them to the sauce will make it taste even better!

Time: *1 hour, 50 minutes*

Serving Size: *4 servings*

Prep Time: *10 minutes*

Cook Time: *1 hour, 40 minutes*

Ingredients:

- 1 tbsp olive oil

- 1 3/4 cups of penne pasta (uncooked)

- 2/3 cup of feta cheese (crumbled)

- 4 cups of pumpkin (peeled, chopped)

- 4 cloves of garlic (unpeeled)

- 4 cups of Roma tomatoes (chopped)

- water (for cooking the pasta)

- parmesan cheese (shaved, for serving)

Directions:

1. Fill a pot with water and place it over medium heat. Bring to a boil.

2. When the water is boiling, add the pasta. Cook according to the directions on the package.

3. After cooking, drain the water and place the cooked pasta in a bowl. Set aside.

4. Preheat your oven to 320°F.

5. In a baking pan, add the tomatoes, pumpkin, and garlic cloves.

6. Drizzle oil over the vegetables, then sprinkle salt and pepper over them. Toss to combine.

7. Place the baking pan in the oven. Roast the vegetables for about 1 hour and 30 minutes.

8. After roasting, take the baking pan out of the oven.

9. Add the roasted pumpkin and tomato to a food processor along with the feta cheese,

10. Squeeze the cloves of garlic out of their skins, then blend everything until you get a smooth texture.

11. Pour the mixture into a saucepan and place it over medium heat.

12. Add the cooked penne pasta to the saucepan and mix well.

13. Spoon the pasta and sauce into a bowl and top with parmesan cheese.

14. Serve immediately.

Sloppy Joe Sauce

Sloppy Joes aren't just messy sandwiches. You can also make pasta that tastes like a sloppy Joe for your little one to enjoy.

Time: 50 *minutes*

Serving Size: 3 *servings*

Prep Time: 20 *minutes*

Cook Time: 30 *minutes*

Ingredients:

- 1/2 cup of cottage cheese

- 1/4 cup of cheddar cheese (shredded)

- 1/2 cup of tomato sauce (canned)

- 1/2 cup of water

- 1/2 cup of tomato paste (canned)

- 1/2 lb ground beef

- 1 cup of small shell pasta (cooked, drained)

- 1 pack of sloppy Joe mix

- cooking spray

Directions:

1. In a saucepan, add the ground beef over medium heat.

2. Cook for about 7 to 8 minutes until the meat isn't pink anymore.

3. Drain the excess oil, then add the water, tomato paste, tomato sauce, and sloppy Joe mix. Stir well.

4. Take the saucepan off the heat, add the pasta, and mix well.

5. Use cooking spray to lightly grease a baking dish and spoon the pasta into it.

6. Top with cottage cheese and cheddar cheese.

7. Place the baking dish in the oven. Bake the pasta for about 33 to 35 minutes at 350°F.

8. After baking, take the baking dish out of the oven.

9. Serve while warm.

Creamy Baked Pasta

Cream-based pasta sauces are delicious and comforting. If you want your little one to try something new, whip up this mouth-watering sauce together.

Time: *30 minutes*

Serving Size: *3 servings*

Prep Time: *10 minutes*

Cook Time: *20 minutes*

Ingredients:

- 1 1/4 tbsp flour

- 1 1/4 tbsp butter (divided)

- 1/2 cup of cheddar cheese (grated)

- 1 cup of milk

- 2/3 cup of button mushrooms (cut in half)

- 1 ¼ cups of farfalle pasta (uncooked)

- 2 slices of ham (thick cut, chopped)

- a bunch of spring onions (finely sliced)

- water (for cooking the pasta)

Directions:

1. Fill a pot with water and place it over medium heat. Bring to a boil.

2. When the water is boiling, add the pasta. Cook according to the directions on the package.

3. After cooking, drain the water and place the cooked pasta in a bowl. Set aside.

4. Preheat your oven to 320°F.

5. In a saucepan, add half of the butter over medium heat.

6. When the butter is hot, add the mushrooms. Cook for about 2 to 3 minutes.

7. Take butter out of the pan and place them in a bowl.

8. Add the rest of the butter to the saucepan along with the onions. Cook for about 1 to 2 minutes.

9. Turn the heat up to medium-high and bring the sauce to a boil.

10. In an oven-safe dish, add the mushrooms and pasta.

11. Pour the sauce into the dish and mix well.

12. Add the ham and some of the cheese, then mix well.

13. Place the dish in the oven. Bake the pasta for about 10 minutes.

14. After baking, take the dish out of the oven.

15. Serve the pasta while it's hot.

Taco Tuesday Fiesta

Classic Beef

Ground beef is the classic filling of tacos. Make this classic dish more interesting by combining it with sweet potatoes, which are very healthy and filling.

Time: *30 minutes*

Serving Size: *3 servings*

Prep Time: *10 minutes*

Cook Time: *20 minutes*

Ingredients:

- 1 tbsp olive oil

- 1/3 cup of water

- 1/2 cup of cherry tomatoes (sliced)

- 1 cup of cheddar cheese (grated; you may also use vegan cheese)

- 1 cup of corn kernels (fresh)

- 1 cup of sweet potato (peeled, grated)

- 1 lb beef mince (lean)

- 1 small onion (peeled, finely chopped)

- 1 small head of lettuce (shredded)

- 1 cucumber (peeled, finely chopped)

- 6 taco shells

- pepper

- salt

- taco sauce or hot sauce (for serving)

Directions:

1. In a pan, add the oil over medium heat.

2. When the oil is hot, add the sweet potato and onion. Cook for about 5 minutes to soften the veggies.

3. Add half of the beef mince, then cook for about 5 minutes while using a wooden spoon to break up any clumps of beef.

4. Use a slotted spoon to transfer the beef and veggies to a bowl.

5. Add the rest of the beef mince to the pan and cook for about 5 minutes.

6. Add the cooked beef and veggies back into the pan.

7. Add water, salt, and pepper, mix well, and bring to a simmer.

8. Scoop the cooked beef and veggies into a serving bowl.

9. Place the rest of the taco ingredients in individual bowls.

10. Serve the taco shells with all the fillings so everyone can enjoy making their own classic beef tacos.

Flaky Fish

The great thing about fish tacos is that you can use any type of white fish for the filling. This recipe features haddock, but you can also use dory, tilapia, or even catfish.

Time: *20 minutes*

Serving Size: *4 servings*

Prep Time: *10 minutes*

Cook Time: *10 minutes*

Ingredients for the tacos:

- 1/2 tsp salt

- 1 tbsp cumin (ground)

- 1 tbsp chili powder

- 2 tbsp vegetable oil

- 8 taco shells (warmed)

- 1 lb haddock (you may use other types of firm white fish)

- toppings like shredded cabbage, guacamole, salsa, grated cheese

Ingredients for the sauce:

- 1/2 tsp chili powder

- 2 tsp lime juice (freshly squeezed)

- 1/2 cup of sour cream

- 1 garlic clove (crushed)

- salt

Directions:

1. In a bowl, add all of the sauce ingredients and mix well. Set aside.

2. In a bowl, add the cumin, salt, and chili powder, then mix well.

3. Coat all the sides of the haddock with the spice mixture.

4. In a skillet, add the oil over medium-high heat.

5. When the oil is hot, add the haddock. Cook each side for about 2 to 3 minutes.

6. Transfer the cooked haddock to a serving plate and allow to cool slightly.

7. Use a fork to gently shred the haddock into chunks.

8. Place the toppings in individual bowls.

9. Serve the taco shells, fish, sauce, and toppings together, and make your own tacos!

Easy Peasy Chicken

The next protein to add to your tacos is chicken. Using different spices for chicken will give different flavor experiences, which your child will surely enjoy.

Time: *20 minutes*

Serving Size: *4 servings*

Prep Time: *5 minutes*

Cook Time: *15 minutes*

Ingredients for the tacos:

- 1/8 tsp black pepper

- 1/4 tsp salt

- 1/4 tsp garlic powder

- 1/4 tsp paprika

- 1/2 tbsp lime juice (freshly squeezed)

- 1/2 tbsp chili powder

- 1 tbsp olive oil

- 1 clove of garlic (minced)

- 1/2 lb chicken thighs (boneless, skinless)

- 4 flour tortillas

Ingredients for the Pico de Gallo:

- 1/8 cup of cilantro (finely chopped)

- 1/2 tsp lime juice (freshly squeezed)

- 1/4 cup of tomato (finely chopped)

- 1/4 cup of onion (finely chopped)

- 1 jalapeño (stem and seeds removed, finely chopped)

- a pinch of salt

- a pinch of pepper

Directions:

1. In a bowl, add the Pico de Gallo ingredients and mix well. Set aside.

2. In a bowl, add all of the taco ingredients except the flour tortillas.

3. Mix well to coat the chicken thighs completely.

4. Heat a pan over medium-high heat.

5. When the pan is hot, add the chicken and cook each side for about 6 to 7 minutes until all pieces are completely cooked through.

6. Transfer the chicken to a chopping board and allow to cool down for about 5 minutes.

7. Chop the chicken thighs into bite-sized pieces.

8. Spoon the chicken into the flour tortillas and top with Pico de Gallo.

9. Serve while hot.

Build Your Own Tacos

To really make Taco Tuesday fun, you can prepare all of the ingredients and lay everything out on the table. Then allow your child and the rest of the family to build their own tacos!

Time: *30 minutes*

Serving Size: *2 servings*

Prep Time: *15 minutes*

Cook Time: *15 minutes*

Ingredients:

- 1 tsp oregano (dried)

- 1 tsp cumin

- 1 tsp paprika

- 1 cup of passata

- 1 cup of cheddar cheese (grated)

- 2 cups of lettuce (shredded)

- 1 avocado (peeled, pitted, chopped)

- 1 1/3 lbs beef mince

- 1 carrot (peeled, grated)

- 2 soft taco shells (warmed)

- 1 tomato (chopped)

- salt

- black pepper

- salsa (for serving)

Directions:

1. Preheat your oven to 350°F.

2. Heat a pan over high heat.

3. When the pan is hot, add the beef mince. Cook until browned while using a wooden spoon to break up any clumps of beef.

4. Add the paprika, oregano, cumin, salt, and pepper, then mix until well combined.

5. Add the passata and mix until well combined.

6. Turn the heat down to low and bring to a simmer.

7. Allow to simmer for about 10 minutes.

8. Spoon the taco filling into a serving bowl, then place the taco shells on a serving platter.

9. Serve immediately so each person can build their own taco!

Mini Taco Cups

Children really like it when you make smaller versions of things for them, and food is no exception. Make these mini taco cups with your child and enjoy every bite!

Time: *30 minutes*

Serving Size: *6 servings*

Prep Time: *10 minutes*

Cook Time: *20 minutes*

Ingredients:

- 2 tsp taco seasoning

- 1 cup of cherry tomatoes (chopped)

- 1 tbsp olive oil

- 2 cups of cheddar cheese (shredded)

- 1 cup of lettuce (shredded)

- 1 lb ground beef

- 6 soft tortillas

- 1/2 onion (chopped)

- black pepper

- kosher salt

- cooking spray

- and sour cream (for serving)

Directions:

1. Preheat your oven to 350°F and use cooking spray to lightly grease a muffin tin.

2. Use a 4-inch circle cookie cutter to cut out small circles from the flour tortillas.

3. Place the circles in the muffin cups and press down with your finger to form little tortilla cups. Set aside.

4. In a skillet, add the oil over medium heat.

5. When the oil is hot, add the onion and cook for about 5 minutes.

6. Add the ground beef and cook until browned while using a wooden spoon to break up any clumps of beef.

7. Add salt, pepper, and taco seasoning, then cook for about 6 minutes.

8. Take the skillet off the heat and drain the oil.

9. Spoon the filling into the taco cups, then top with shredded cheese.

10. Place the muffin tin in the oven. Bake the taco cups for about 10 minutes.

11. After baking, take the muffin tin out of the oven.

12. Top each taco cup with tomatoes, lettuce, and sour cream.

13. Serve while hot.

Chapter 6:

Sweet Tooth Treats

Children love sweet treats! Rather than preventing your child from eating sweets all the time, it's better to make healthy sweet treats with them. While doing this, you can introduce the importance of healthy eating and how you can use nutritious ingredients to make the tasty treats they love to eat.

Cookie Decorating Bonanza

Fluffy and Snowy

These cheesecake cookies are fluffy, snowy, and perfectly sweet. They're easy to make and a lot of fun to eat!

Time: 30 minutes (cooling time not included)

Serving Size: 5 servings

Prep Time: 18 minutes

Cook Time: 12 minutes

Ingredients:

- 1/2 tsp baking powder

- 1/4 tsp kosher salt

- 1/8 cup of sugar (powdered)

- 1/8 cup of butter (unsalted, softened)

- 1/3 cup of cream cheese (softened)

- 3/4 cup of all-purpose flour

- 1/3 cup of sugar (granulated)

- 15 maraschino cherries (stems removed)

- 1 egg

Directions:

1. Preheat your oven to 350°F and use a sheet of parchment paper to line a baking sheet.

2. In a bowl, add the butter, cream cheese, and granulated sugar. Use an electric mixer to combine the ingredients on the medium-low setting until you get a smooth texture.

3. Add the egg and continue to beat until everything is well combined.

4. In another bowl, add the baking powder, flour, and salt, then whisk to combine.

5. Slowly add the flour mixture into the bowl with the cream cheese while beating at a low speed.

6. Scoop dollops of the batter onto the baking sheet, making sure that there is enough space between each cookie.

7. Place the baking sheet in the oven and bake the cookies for about 12 minutes.

8. After baking, take the baking sheet out of the oven.

9. Use the back of a spoon to press the center of the cookies while they are still hot to make a well, then allow the cookies to cool down for about 30 minutes.

10. Place a cherry in the well that you have made in each cookie, then dust the tops of the cookies with powdered sugar.

11. Serve.

Icing and Sprinkles

Children love to add sprinkles and icing on cakes and cookies! Here is a recipe to make with your child that's fun and colorful.

Time: *30 minutes*

Serving Size: *4 servings*

Prep Time: *30 minutes*

Cook Time: *no cooking time*

Ingredients:

- 1/2 tsp peppermint extract

- 1 1/3 cups of icing sugar

- 4 large cookies

- rainbow sprinkles

- water (to add to the icing)

Directions:

1. In a bowl, add the icing sugar and peppermint extract with enough water to create a thick, fluffy icing.

2. Use a dull knife to spread the icing all over the surface of the cookies.

3. Top each cookie with rainbow sprinkles.

4. Serve.

Glazed Doughnut

There's something so fun about foods that look like other things. These cute cookies look like donuts but are delightfully crunchy and thin.

Time: *35 minutes (chilling time not included)*

Serving Size: *6 servings*

Prep Time: *20 minutes*

Cook Time: *15 minutes*

Ingredients:

- 1/3 tsp cinnamon (ground)

- 1/4 tsp nutmeg (ground)

- 1 tsp baking powder

- 1 1/2 tbsp heavy cream

- 1 tsp vanilla extract (divided)

- 1 cup of confectioners' sugar

- 1/2 cup of sugar (granulated)

- 1 1/2 cups of all-purpose flour

- 1 egg

- 1 1/2 drops of red food coloring

- 1 stick of butter (unsalted, at room temperature)

- rainbow sprinkles

- a pinch of sea salt

Directions:

1. In a bowl, add the flour, cinnamon, nutmeg, baking powder, and salt, then whisk well.

2. In another bowl, add the granulated sugar and butter. Use an electric mixer to cream the butter and sugar for about 4 minutes to get a fluffy and light texture.

3. Add the egg and half of the vanilla extract, then mix until well combined.

4. Add the flour mixture into the bowl and continue to blend until you form a dough.

5. Use your hands to form the dough into a ball, then flatten it into a disc.

6. Use cling wrap to cover the disc, then place it in the refrigerator to chill for about 1 hour.

7. After chilling, take the dough disc out of the refrigerator and unwrap it.

8. Preheat your oven to 350°F and use a sheet of parchment paper to line a baking sheet.

9. Roll out the dough on a lightly floured surface, then use a cookie cutter to cut out circular donut-sized cookies.

10. Use a smaller cookie cutter to cut out a circle in the middle of each cookie.

11. Place the cookies on the baking sheet, making sure that there is enough space between each cookie.

12. Place the baking sheet in the oven. Bake the cookies for about 12 to 15 minutes.

13. After baking, take the baking sheet out of the oven and allow the cookies to cool down completely.

14. When the cookies have cooled down, prepare the donut glaze. In a bowl, add the cream, confectioners' sugar, food coloring, and the rest of the vanilla extract, then mix well.

15. Dip one of the cookies face-down into the bowl with the glaze, turn it over, and place it on a wire rack.

16. Top with rainbow sprinkles.

17. Repeat the glazing steps for the rest of the cookies.

18. Allow the glaze to harden before serving.

Colorful Marshmallows

This recipe will give you cookies that are colorful, pretty, and really tasty too. This simple recipe is a breeze to make and your child will surely enjoy making them.

Time: *20 minutes (chilling time not included)*

Serving Size: *4 servings*

Prep Time: *20 minutes*

Cook Time: *no cooking time*

Ingredients:

- 4 tbsp butter

- 1 1/4 cups of colorful mini marshmallows

- 1 1/2 cups of chocolate pieces (semi-sweet)

- 1 1/2 cups of walnuts (chopped)

- 2 eggs (beaten)

- confectioners' sugar

Directions:

1. In a saucepan, add the butter and chocolate pieces over low heat.

2. Heat while mixing until the chocolate melts and combines with the butter.

3. When the chocolate has melted, take the saucepan off the heat.

4. Add the eggs and mix to combine, then allow the mixture to cool down slightly.

5. In a bowl, add the nuts and marshmallows, then mix well.

6. Pour the melted chocolate mixture into the bowl with the nuts and marshmallows, then mix to combine.

7. Use your hands to take portions of the mixture and form each portion into a cookie shape.

8. Place the cookies on the baking sheet, then place in the refrigerator to chill for a minimum of 15 minutes.

9. Serve when the cookies have firmed up.

Out of This World!

These planet cookies look amazing and they taste great too. Children like to make cool things and when those things are edible, making them is much more fun!

Time: *40 minutes*

Serving Size: *4 servings*

Prep Time: *28 minutes*

Cook Time: *12 minutes*

Ingredients:

- 1/2 tsp vanilla extract

- 1/4 cup of golden caster sugar

- 1/4 cup of butter (unsalted, softened)

- 1/2 cup of all-purpose flour

- 1 egg (lightly beaten)

- 1/2 cup of royal icing sugar

- gold edible glitter

- gel food coloring (red, orange, yellow, green, blue, and black)

- water (to make the icing)

Directions:

1. Preheat your oven to 350°F, and use a sheet of parchment paper to line a baking sheet.

2. In a bowl, add the sugar and butter, then use an electric beater to combine the ingredients until you get a fluffy and pale mixture.

3. Slowly beat the vanilla extract and egg into the mixture.

4. Add the flour, then continue mixing until you form a dough.

5. Roll the dough on a lightly floured surface, then use circle-shaped cookie cutters to cut 8 cookies of different sizes.

6. Transfer the cookies to the baking sheet, making sure that there is enough space between each cookie.

7. Place the baking sheet in the oven. Bake the cookies for about 10 to 12 minutes.

8. After baking, take the baking sheet out of the oven.

9. Transfer the cookies to a wire rack to cool down completely.

10. When the cookies have cooled down, prepare the icing. In a bowl add the icing sugar with enough water to make a spreadable and smooth icing.

11. Divide the icing into 6 bowls and add food coloring gel to each. Mix until the icing becomes colored.

12. Spread different colors of icing all over the surfaces of the cookies. You can even mix and match different colors together to make the cookies look like planets.

13. Sprinkle edible glitter over the cookies to make them sparkly.

14. Allow the icing to set before serving.

Cupcake Decorating Showcase

Googly-Eyed Aliens

Children really enjoy cooking when they can make cute and funny foods. Here is one example of a cupcake that looks like a googly-eyed alien!

Time: 20 *minutes*

Serving Size: 6 *servings*

Prep Time: 20 *minutes*

Cook Time: *no cooking time*

Ingredients:

- 1/4 cup of purple-colored sprinkles

- 1/2 cup of brown frosting

- 2 cups of vanilla frosting

- 6 cupcakes (chocolate or vanilla, cooked)

- 12 large marshmallows

- 12 M&M's minis

- 24 miniature marshmallows

- food coloring (neon green)

Directions:

1. Add some neon green food coloring to the vanilla frosting and mix well.

2. Spread frosting on top of the cupcakes, then top with purple-colored sprinkles.

3. Pipe a dot of brown frosting onto one of the large marshmallows, then stick a mini M&M on it to make an "eye." Do this for the rest of the large marshmallows.

4. Pierce toothpicks into the marshmallows, then add them to the cupcakes.

5. Decorate the cupcakes with mini marshmallows and serve.

Birthday Surprise

Have you ever tried serving cupcakes for your child's birthday? Here is a recipe for fun and colorful birthday cupcakes to make with your child!

Time: *50 minutes*

Serving Size: *12 servings*

Prep Time: *20 minutes*

Cook Time: *30 minutes*

Ingredients:

- 1/2 tsp baking soda

- 1/2 tsp almond extract

- 1/2 tsp salt

- 1 tsp vanilla extract

- 3/4 tsp baking powder

- 1/3 cup of sour cream

- 1/8 cup rainbow sprinkles (divided)

- 1/2 cup of butter (salted)

- 3/4 cup of sugar

- 1/2 cup of milk

- 1 cup of buttercream frosting

- 1 large egg

- 1 1/4 cups of cake flour

- cooking spray

Directions:

1. Preheat your oven to 350°F and use cooking spray to lightly grease a muffin tin.

2. In a bowl, add the sugar and butter, then use an electric mixer to beat until you get a smooth texture.

3. Add the vanilla extract, almond extract, sour cream, and milk, then blend until you get a smooth texture.

4. Add baking powder, baking soda, cake flour, salt, and half of the rainbow sprinkles, then beat until well combined and you get a smooth batter.

5. Pour the batter into the muffin cups, making sure that you don't fill them to the brim.

6. Place the muffin tin in the oven and bake the muffins for about 25 to 30 minutes.

7. After baking, take the muffin tin out of the oven, and allow the muffins to cool down completely.

8. When the muffins have cooled down, top each of them with buttercream frosting and rainbow sprinkles.

9. Serve.

Rainbow Unicorn

Little girls love unicorn cupcakes, and little boys will enjoy making them too. Whip up a batch of cupcakes and see who can make the prettiest unicorn in the bunch!

Time: 50 *minutes*

Serving Size: 12 *cupcakes*

Prep Time: *30 minutes*

Cook Time: *20 minutes*

Ingredients for the cupcakes:

- 2/3 cup of butter (melted)

- 3/4 cup of self-rising flour

- 3/4 cup of white caster sugar

- 2 eggs

- cooking spray

Ingredients for the unicorn topping:

- 1/4 tsp vanilla extract

- 4 tsp milk

- 1 1/4 cups of butter (softened)

- 1 2/3 cups of icing sugar

- food coloring (pink, purple, and blue)

- various sprinkles and sweets like chocolate stars, chocolate chips, M&M minis, and more

Ingredients for the syrup:

- 1 tsp vanilla extract

- 3 tbsp maple syrup

Directions:

1. Preheat your oven to 350°F and use cooking spray to lightly grease a muffin tray.

2. In a bowl, add the vanilla extract and maple syrup, then mix well. Set aside.

3. Add all of the cupcake ingredients to another bowl, then beat with an electric mixer until you have a smooth and pale batter.

4. Pour the batter into the muffin cups, making sure that you don't fill them to the brim.

5. Place the muffin tin in the oven and bake the muffins for about 20 minutes.

6. After baking, take the muffin tin out of the oven.

7. Place the muffins on a wire rack to cool down completely.

8. While the muffins are cooling, prepare the icing. In a bowl, add the icing sugar, milk, vanilla extract, and butter, then whisk until smooth.

9. Divide the frosting into 2, then divide 1/2 of the frosting into 3.

10. Add food coloring to the 3 portions of frosting in a bowl, then mix well to make frosting with different colors.

11. When the muffins have cooled down, decorate them with colored frosting, sprinkles, and sweets to make unicorn cupcakes.

12. After decorating, drizzle vanilla syrup over the cupcakes and serve.

Choco Paw Prints

If you have a pet at home or if your child loves animals, these chocolate cupcakes will surely put a smile on their face. They're easy to make and tasty, too!

Time: *40 minutes*

Serving Size: *12 cupcakes*

Prep Time: *20 minutes*

Cook Time: *20 minutes*

Ingredients:

- 1 cup of vanilla frosting

- 2 cups of coconut (shredded, sweetened)

- 1 box of chocolate-flavored cupcake mix along with the ingredients needed to make the cupcakes.

- 12 Oreos

- 48 brown-colored M&Ms

- cooking spray

Directions:

1. Preheat your oven to 350°F and use cooking spray to lightly grease a muffin tin.

2. Follow the directions on the box of the chocolate cupcake mix to make the cupcake batter.

3. Pour the batter into the muffin cups, making sure that you don't fill them to the brim.

4. Place the muffin tin in the oven and bake the cupcakes for about 20 minutes or as indicated on the box.

5. After baking, take the muffin tin out of the oven, and transfer the muffins to a wire rack to cool down completely.

6. When the muffins have cooled down completely, top each one with a dollop of vanilla frosting.

7. Arrange the Oreos and M&Ms on the frosting to look like paw prints, then top with shredded coconut.

8. Serve.

Ice Cream Cones

These cool cupcakes look like ice cream cones complete with rainbow sprinkles. They're fun, colorful, and they taste delicious too!

Time: 40 *minutes*

Serving Size: 12 *servings*

Prep Time: 20 *minutes*

Cook Time: 20 *minutes*

Ingredients for the cupcakes:

- 1 box of vanilla cupcake mix along with the ingredients needed to make the cupcakes.

- 12 ice cream cake cones

- cooking spray

Ingredients for the frosting:

- 1 tsp vanilla extract

- 1/8 cup of milk

- 1/4 cup of shortening

- 1/2 cup of butter (softened)

- 3 cups of confectioners' sugar

- rainbow sprinkles

Directions:

1. Preheat your oven to 350°F and use cooking spray to lightly grease a muffin tin.

2. Follow the directions on the box of the chocolate cupcake mix to make the cupcake batter.

3. Pour the batter into the muffin cups, making sure that you don't fill them to the brim.

4. Place the muffin tin in the oven and bake the cupcakes for about 20 minutes or as indicated on the box.

5. After baking, take the muffin tin out of the oven, and transfer the muffins to a wire rack to cool down completely.

6. While the muffins are cooling down, make the frosting. In a bowl, add the shortening and butter, then use an electric mixer to beat until you get a smooth texture.

7. Continue to beat while you slowly add the vanilla extract, milk, and confectioner sugar.

8. Keep beating until you can form smooth and soft peaks with the frosting.

9. When the muffins have cooled down, insert them into the holes of the cones.

10. Spread frosting all over the surface of the cupcakes, then top with rainbow sprinkles.

11. Serve.

Fruity Ice Cream Sundae Bar

Summer Fruits

Using fresh fruits to make ice cream is a great way to add healthy foods into your child's diet. The best part is, there are many fruits out there for you to choose from!

Time: 25 minutes

Serving Size: 4 servings

Prep Time: 20 minutes

Cook Time: 5 minutes

Ingredients for the ice cream:

- 2 tbsp icing sugar

- 2/3 cup of double cream

- 4 nectarines (peeled, chopped into chunks)

- 4 scoops of ice cream (vanilla flavor)

- 4 scoops of sorbet (berry flavor)

- 4 strawberries

- 8 strawberries (stems removed, chopped)

Ingredients for the brittle:

- 1/3 cup of caster sugar

- 1/3 cup of macadamia nuts (toasted)

- sunflower oil

Ingredients for the sauce:

- 1 tbsp icing sugar

- 1 1/4 cups of strawberries (stems removed)

Directions:

1. Use sunflower oil to lightly grease a baking sheet, then set aside.

2. In a pan, add the caster sugar over low heat. Stir until the sugar dissolves completely.

3. Add the macadamia nuts and mix until well incorporated.

4. Pour the mixture onto the baking sheet and allow the brittle to harden.

5. When the brittle has hardened, snap it into small pieces.

6. Add the brittle to a food processor, then pulse until you get coarse crumbs.

7. Transfer the crumbs to a bowl and set aside.

8. Add the strawberries for the sauce to a food processor, then blend until smooth.

9. Pour the blended strawberries into a bowl through a sieve.

10. Add the icing sugar, mix well, and set aside.

11. In a bowl, add the cream and icing sugar, then whip until you can form soft peaks.

12. In a glass, add layers of fruit, crumbs, sorbet, ice cream, and strawberry sauce.

13. Repeat the assembling steps for all of the servings.

14. Top each serving with whipped cream, brittle crumbs, and 1 strawberry each.

Tropical Flavors

Mixing tropical flavors will surely delight your child's taste buds. You can even use this time as a learning opportunity to teach your child about different types of tropical fruits from around the world.

Time: *5 minutes (chilling time not included)*

Serving Size: *2 servings*

Prep Time: *5 minutes*

Cook Time: *no cooking time*

Ingredients:

- 1/4 cup of pineapple (minced)

- 1/4 cup of coconut flakes (toasted)

- 2 scoops of ice cream (vanilla flavor)

- 1/4 cup of strawberries (stems removed, chopped)

- 2 graham crackers

- 1 banana (peeled, sliced)

- a drizzle of chocolate sauce

- a sprinkle of sugar

Directions:

1. In an airtight container, add the strawberries, then sprinkle some sugar over them.

2. Cover the container with a lid and shake the container.

3. Place the container in the refrigerator overnight for the strawberries to release their juices.

4. After chilling, take the container with strawberries out of the oven.

5. Prepare 2 bowls and add 1 scoop of ice cream to each of them.

6. Top with pineapples, bananas, and strawberries.

7. Drizzle chocolate sauce over the ice cream, then top with coconut flakes and peanuts.

8. Place the graham cracker right next to the scoop of ice cream.

9. Serve immediately.

Tutti Fruity

Chopping up fruits and mixing them up to make a delicious and colorful ice cream is a lot of fun for kids. It's a lot of fun to make and it's a lot of fun to eat too!

Time: *10 minutes*

Serving Size: *4 servings*

Prep Time: *10 minutes*

Cook Time: *no cooking time*

Ingredients:

- 1/4 cup of blueberries (fresh)

- 1/2 cup of strawberries (stems removed, cut in half)

- 4 scoops of ice cream (vanilla flavor)

- 1 apple (cored, roughly chopped)

- 1 banana (peeled, sliced)

- 1 kiwi (peeled, roughly chopped)

- 1 nectarine (peeled, roughly chopped)

- 1 orange (peeled, roughly chopped)

- 1 sprig of mint (leaves picked)

Directions:

1. In a bowl, add all of the fruits and mix well.

2. Spoon the mixed fruits into 4 bowls, then top each bowl with a scoop of ice cream.

3. Top each scoop of ice cream with some mint leaves.

4. Serve immediately.

Coconut and Pineapple

Coconuts and pineapples are tropical fruits that go well with everything! These are refreshing fruits that look good in desserts and taste even better.

Time: 10 *minutes*

Serving Size: 4 *servings*

Prep Time: 5 *minutes*

Cook Time: 5 *minutes*

Ingredients:

- 2 tbsp golden caster sugar

- 3 tbsp coconut syrup

- 2 cups of pineapple (fresh, chopped into chunks)

- 8 scoops of ice cream (coconut flavor)

- 8 ginger biscuits (crumbled)

- a handful of coconut (dried, sliced)

Directions:

1. In a pan, add the coconut syrup, sugar, and pineapple chunks over high heat.

2. Cook for about 5 minutes until the sugar dissolves.

3. Take the pan off the heat and allow the pineapple to cool down.

4. Spoon some crumbled biscuits into the bottom of 4 bowls, then top with the cooked pineapple.

5. Add a scoop of ice cream to each bowl, then top with dried coconut.

6. Serve immediately.

Fudgy Bananas

This is a super simple ice cream dessert that include bananas, one of the most common fruits that children love. The best part is, bananas are soft, so you can just guide your child when making this sweet treat.

Time: *30 minutes (freezing time not included)*

Serving Size: *4 servings*

Prep Time: *25 minutes*

Cook Time: *5 minutes*

Ingredients for the bananas:

- 1/3 cup of golden caster sugar

- 2 cups of soy yogurt

- 4 bananas (very ripe)

- a handful of pecans (toasted, chopped)

Ingredients for the sauce:

- 2 tbsp maple syrup

- 8 tbsp soy cream

- 1/3 cup of chocolate spread (preferably dairy-free)

- 2/3 cup of light muscovado sugar

Directions:

1. Add the bananas, sugar, and soy yogurt to a food processor and process until smooth and creamy.

2. Transfer the mixture into an airtight container with a lid and place in the freezer for about 8 hours. Every 2 hours or so, whip the mixture to prevent the formation of ice crystals.

3. When the ice cream is ready, prepare the sauce. In a saucepan, add the chocolate sauce over medium heat.

4. When the chocolate spread has melted, add the syrup and sugar, then mix well until all of the sugar has dissolved.

5. Stir the cream into the chocolate mixture and bring to a boil.

6. Allow to boil for about 2 to 3 minutes for the sauce to thicken.

7. Pour the sauce into a bowl and allow it to cool down.

8. Add 1 scoop of ice cream into 4 bowls, then drizzle with chocolate sauce on top.

9. Top with pecans and serve immediately.

Chapter 7:

Global Flavors Exploration

Introducing your child to different cuisines is a wonderful learning experience for them. Rather than just cooking exotic meals for your child, include them in the cooking process! That way, they can learn about different ingredients and how these are used to make interesting dishes from all over the world.

Easy Sushi Rolls for Kids

Sandwich Roll

Have you ever served sandwiches to your child in the form of sushi rolls? Your child will surely have fun making these sandwich rolls and adding their favorite toppings. Then you can enjoy them together.

Time: 10 *minutes*

Serving Size: 2 *servings*

Prep Time: 10 *minutes*

Cook Time: *no cooking time*

Ingredients:

- 1/2 tsp mayonnaise

- 1/2 tsp mustard

- 1 small cucumber (peeled, sliced into matchsticks)

- 1 thin carrot stick (peeled, sliced into matchsticks)

- 2 cheese sticks

- 2 slices of bread (preferably whole grain)

- 4 slices of turkey ham

Directions:

1. Use a knife to slice off the crusts of the bread slices, then use a rolling pin to flatten them.

2. Spread mustard and mayonnaise all over one side of the bread slices.

3. Place 2 slices of turkey ham on each slice of bread.

4. Arrange the carrots, cucumber, and cheese sticks at the bottom of the turkey slices.

5. Start rolling the slice of bread tightly from the bottom. Make sure to squeeze everything together as you roll so that everything will get squeezed together.

6. When you reach the end, press along the edge of the bread to seal the seam.

7. Use a sharp knife to slice the sandwich rolls, then arrange them on a platter.

8. Serve.

PB&J Roll

Peanut butter and jelly is a classic combination that all children love. Here, instead of jelly, you will use apples and raisings in the form of a sushi roll to delight your child with each bite!

Time: *10 minutes*

Serving Size: *2 servings*

Prep Time: *10 minutes*

Cook Time: *no cooking time*

Ingredients:

- 1/4 cup of raisins

- 2 slices of bread (preferably whole wheat)

- 1 apple (cored, sliced into thin strips)

- 1/2 cup of peanut butter

- juice of 1/2 lemon

Directions:

1. In a bowl, add the apple strips and lemon juice, then toss to combine.

2. Allow to sit while you prepare the bread.

3. Use a knife to slice off the crusts of the bread slices, then use a rolling pin to flatten them.

4. Spread peanut butter all over the bread slices.

5. Arrange the apple slices at the bottom of each bread slice, then top with raisins.

6. Start rolling the slice of bread tightly from the bottom. Make sure to squeeze everything together as you roll so that everything will get squeezed together.

7. When you reach the end, press along the edge of the bread to seal the seam.

8. Use a sharp knife to slice the sandwich rolls, then arrange them on a platter.

9. Serve.

Avocado and Veggie Roll

The great thing about sushi rolls is that you can use different ingredients to make them. Since sushi rolls are interesting for children, you can use them to encourage your child to eat more fruits and veggies.

Time: *20 minutes*

Serving Size: *3 servings*

Prep Time: *10 minutes*

Cook Time: *10 minutes*

Ingredients for the rice:

- 1 tbsp avocado oil

- 1 tsp sea salt

- 2 3/4 cups of sushi rice (cooked)

- 1 tbsp mirin

Ingredients for the sushi:

- 1 tbsp water

- 1/4 tsp sea salt

- 1 small cucumber (sliced into thin strips)

- 2 small carrots (sliced into thin strips)

- 2 avocados (peeled, pitted, sliced)

- 3 big nori sheets

Directions:

1. In a pan, add the avocado oil over medium-high heat.

2. When the oil is hot, add the sushi rice, mirin, and salt. Cook for about 8 minutes while mixing well.

3. Spoon the rice into the nori sheets and use a spatula to spread the rice all over the nori sheets in a flat and even layer.

4. Add the avocado slices and salt to a bowl, then use a fork to mix and mash well.

5. Spread avocado all over the latter of sushi rice.

6. Arrange the carrot and cucumber slices at the bottom of each nori sheet.

7. Start rolling the nori sheet tightly from the bottom. Make sure to squeeze everything together as you roll so that everything will get squeezed together.

8. When you reach the end, dip your finger in water and wet the edge of the nori sheet to seal the seam.

9. Use a sharp knife to slice the sandwich rolls, then arrange them on a platter.

10. Serve.

California Roll

California maki is one of the more popular types of sushi rolls. If you want to introduce your child to eating sushi, it would be nice to teach them how to make it with you. Here is a simple recipe for you to follow.

Time: *30 minutes*

Serving Size: *4 servings*

Prep Time: *10 minutes*

Cook Time: *20 minutes*

Ingredients for the omelet:

- 1/4 tsp salt

- 1/2 tsp oil

- 1/2 tsp sugar

- 1 tsp light soy sauce

- 1 tsp mirin

- 4 eggs

Ingredients for the rest of the sushi:

- 1 tbsp water

- 3 cups of sushi rice (cooked)

- 1 cucumber (peeled, sliced thinly)

- 2 carrots (blanched, peeled, sliced thinly)

- 2 mangoes (peeled, sliced thinly)

- 4 large nori sheets

Directions:

1. In a bowl, add all of the omelet ingredients except for the oil, and whisk well.

2. In a pan, add the oil over low heat.

3. When the oil is hot, pour the egg mixture into the pan until the surface dries up.

4. Flip the omelet over and cook the other side too.

5. After cooking, transfer the omelet to a plate and allow it to cool down.

6. When the omelet has cooled down, slice it into thin strips.

7. Spoon the rice into the nori sheets and use a spatula to spread it in a flat and even layer.

8. Arrange the omelet, carrot, cucumber, and mango slices at the bottom of each nori sheet.

9. Start rolling the nori sheet tightly from the bottom. Make sure to squeeze everything together as you roll so that everything will get squeezed together.

10. When you reach the end, dip your finger in water and wet the edge of the nori sheet to seal the seam.

11. Use a sharp knife to slice the sandwich rolls, then arrange them on a platter.

12. Serve.

Sweet Banana Rolls

For a delicious and colorful dessert, give this sushi a try. Your child will enjoy making these sweet banana rolls as much as you will both enjoy eating them once they are chilled and ready.

Time: 10 *minutes (chilling time not included)*

Serving Size: 4 *servings*

Prep Time: 10 *minutes*

Cook Time: *no cooking time*

Ingredients:

- 1/2 cup of Fruity Pebble cereal (or any of your child's favorite cereal)

- 1/2 cup of blackberries (fresh)

- 4 bananas (peeled, sliced in half crosswise)

- 1/2 cup of Greek yogurt (plain)

Directions:

1. Add the blackberries and cereal to a shallow dish and mix to combine.

2. Spread Greek yogurt all over the banana halves until they are completely coated.

3. Roll the banana halves in the blackberry and cereal mix, then place them on a plate.

4. Place the plate in the refrigerator to chill for about 15 minutes.

5. When ready to serve. Take the plate out of the refrigerator.

6. Use a sharp knife to slice the banana halves.

7. Serve.

Mini Tacos From Around the World

Mexican Classic

Since tacos are a classic Mexican treat, let's start with traditional Mexican tacos. Introduce your child to new flavors and dishes by inviting them to make different dishes like these and enjoying them with the whole family.

Time: *35 minutes*

Serving Size: *4 servings*

Prep Time: *15 minutes*

Cook Time: *20 minutes*

Ingredients:

- 1/2 tsp onion powder

- 1/2 tsp garlic powder

- 1 tsp cumin

- 1 tsp smoked paprika

- 1 tsp oregano (dried)

- 1 tbsp vegetable oil

- 1 tbsp chili powder

- 1/4 cup of lettuce (shredded)

- 1/4 cup of red onion (diced)

- 1/4 cup of tomato (diced)

- 1 lb ground beef (lean)

- 1/2 cup of tomato sauce (canned)

- 1 avocado (peeled, pitted, sliced)

- 8 mini taco shells

- salt

- pepper

- sour cream (for serving)

- cheddar cheese (shredded, for garnish)

Directions:

1. Place a skillet on the stove over medium-high heat.

2. When the skillet is hot, add the beef. Cook for about 8 to 10 minutes until the beef is no longer pink.

3. Add the tomato sauce, spices, and seasonings, then cook for about 5 to 7 minutes.

4. Drain and discard the excess oil.

5. Spoon some ground beef into each of the mini taco shells, then top with tomatoes, onion, avocado, and lettuce.

6. Top each taco with cheese and a dollop of sour cream.

7. Serve immediately.

Korean Pickled

Have you ever tried pickled Korean-style tacos. If this is your first time, you can make these mini tacos with your child, then take your first bite together. You will definitely enjoy this variation of the Mexican classic.

Time: *20 minutes*

Serving Size: *4 servings*

Prep Time: *10 minutes*

Cook Time: *10 minutes*

Ingredients:

- 1 tsp caster sugar

- 1/2 tsp chili flakes

- 1 tbsp vegetable oil

- 2 tsp sesame seeds (toasted)

- 2 tbsp ginger (fresh, grated)

- 2 tbsp rice wine vinegar

- 2 tbsp light soy sauce

- 1/4 cup of lettuce (shredded)

- 1/2 cup of cilantro leaves (fresh)

- 1/4 cup of sweet chili sauce

- 1 cucumber (thinly sliced)

- 1 carrot (thinly sliced)

- 1 small red onion (thinly sliced)

- 3 cloves of garlic (crushed)

- 2 beef porterhouse steaks

- 8 mini taco shells

Directions:

1. In a bowl, add the ginger, garlic, sweet chili sauce, chili flakes, and steaks.

2. Turn the steaks over to coat them with the marinade.

3. Cover the bowl and allow the steaks to marinate for about 20 minutes.

4. In another bowl, add the vinegar, sugar, onion, cucumber, and carrot, then toss to combine all of the ingredients together.

5. Cover the bowl and allow to sit for about 20 minutes.

6. After marinating, transfer the steaks to a plate and brush oil over both sides.

7. Heat a grill pan over high heat.

8. When the grill pan is hot, add the steaks and cook each side for about 2 minutes or until your desired doneness.

9. After cooking, transfer the steaks to a plate and allow them to rest for about 5 minutes.

10. After resting, use a sharp knife to slice the steaks into thin strips.

11. Add some steak slices to the bottom of each mini taco shell, then add pickled veggies on top.

12. Top each mini taco with lettuce, sesame seeds, and cilantro leaves.

13. Serve immediately.

Spiced Peruvian

Have you ever tried Peruvian tacos? Here is a yummy and unique variation of mini tacos for you to try at home. This time, you will be baking the mini tacos to make them deliciously warm and hearty.

Time: *30 minutes*

Serving Size: *4 servings*

Prep Time: *15 minutes*

Cook Time: *15 minutes*

Ingredients:

- 2 tsp cilantro (ground)

- 2 tsp cumin (ground)

- 1/4 cup of green olives (pitted, chopped)

- 1/4 cup of plums (dried, pitted, sliced)

- 1/2 cup of Cotija cheese (shredded)

- 1/2 cup of onion (chopped)

- 1 cup of tomatoes (canned, diced)

- 1 lb ground chicken

- 1 potato (peeled, finely chopped)

- 8 mini taco shells

Directions:

1. Preheat your oven to 350°F.

2. In a skillet, add the onion and chicken over medium-high heat. Cook until the ground chicken is no longer pink.

3. Drain any excess oil from the skillet.

4. Add the cumin, cilantro, and salt, then cook for about 1 to 2 minutes while stirring frequently.

5. Add the potatoes, plums, tomatoes, and olives.

6. Stir everything together and bring the mixture to a boil.

7. When the mixture is boiling, turn the heat down to medium.

8. Simmer for about 12 to 15 minutes until the potatoes are fork-tender and most of the liquid has evaporated.

9. Take the skillet off the heat.

10. Spoon the mixture into the bottom of each mini taco shell, top with cheese, and place on a baking sheet.

11. Place the baking sheet in the oven and bake the tacos for about 5 minutes to crisp them up and melt the cheese.

12. After baking, take the baking sheet out of the oven.

13. Serve the mini tacos while hot.

Sour and Spicy Thai

For another Asian variation, try these sour and spicy Thai-style mini tacos. Thai food typically contains fresh and bright ingredients, and this dish is no exception. Serve them to impress your whole family, including the children.

Time: *2 hours, 25 minutes*

Serving Size: *8 servings*

Prep Time: *25 minutes*

Cook Time: *2 hours*

Ingredients for the tacos:

- 1 tbsp ginger (fresh, grated)

- 1/8 tsp red pepper flakes

- 1 tbsp honey

- 1/8 cup of soy sauce

- 1/8 cup of lime juice (freshly squeezed)

- 2 cloves of garlic (minced)

- 1 pork tenderloin (fat trimmed off)

- 16 mini taco shells

Ingredients for the slaw:

- 1/3 cup of cilantro (fresh, chopped)

- 1 1/2 tbsp sriracha sauce

- 3/4 cup of red cabbage (finely shredded)

- 1/3 cup of mayonnaise

- 2 cloves of garlic (minced)

- 2 cups of cabbage and carrot blend (prepared coleslaw mix, shredded)

- salt

- black pepper

Directions:

1. Add all the slaw ingredients to a bowl and mix well. Set aside.

2. In a slow cooker, add the pork tenderloin.

3. In a bowl, add the rest of the taco ingredients except for the mini taco shells, and mix well.

4. Pour the mixture over the meat into the slow cooker.

5. Set the slow cooker on high, close the lid, and cook the meat for about 2 hours.

6. After cooking, open the slow cooker and transfer the meat to a bowl.

7. Use a fork to shred the meat, then mix it with the cooking liquid from the slow cooker.

8. Add some pork to the bottom of each mini taco shell and top with slaw.

9. Serve immediately after assembling.

Plant-Based

Tacos don't have to contain meat. Even if you use plant-based ingredients, you can still make tasty tacos that your child will enjoy building and eating. Here is a recipe for plant-based tacos that's a winner!

Time: *2 hours, 20 minutes*

Serving Size: *5 servings*

Prep Time: *20 minutes*

Cook Time: *2 hours*

Ingredients to cook:

- 2 tbsp taco seasoning

- 1/4 tsp salt

- 3 tbsp olive oil

- 2 cups of whole corn kernels (fresh)

- 1/4 cup of sweet onion (chopped)

- 2 chipotle peppers in adobo sauce (canned, finely chopped)

- 4 cups of cauliflower florets

Other ingredients:

- 1/2 cup of green onions (chopped)

- 1/4 cup of cilantro (fresh, chopped)

- 1 cup of cucumber (chopped)

- 1 jalapeño (seeds and stem removed, finely chopped)

- 1 clove of garlic (minced)

- 1 lime (sliced into wedges)

- 10 mini taco shells

- 2 avocados (peeled, pitted, sliced)

- queso fresco (crumbled, for serving)

Directions:

1. In a slow cooker, add all of the ingredients to cook, and mix well.

2. Set the slow cooker to high, close the lid, and cook the veggies for about 2 hours, only stirring everything once halfway through the cooking time.

3. In a bowl, add the cilantro, green onions, cucumber, garlic, and jalapeño.

4. Squeeze the juice from 2 of the lime wedges into the bowl, then mix everything well. Set aside.

5. Open the lid of the slow cooker and transfer the contents to a bowl.

6. Scoop some filling into each of the mini taco shells, then top with the fresh vegetable mixture.

7. Top each mini taco with avocado slices and crumbled cheese.

8. Serve immediately with lime wedges on the side.

Kid-Friendly Stir-Fry Adventure

Chicken and Veggies

Stir-frying involves cooking various ingredients in a pan or wok over a stove. You have to help your child through these cooking steps, especially if it is their first time to cook. While making this recipe, try to introduce the kitchen safety rules too.

Time: *30 minutes*

Serving Size: *3 servings*

Prep Time: *15 minutes*

Cook Time: *15 minutes*

Ingredients for the sauce:

- 1/2 tbsp apple cider vinegar

- 1/2 tsp ginger (fresh, grated)

- 3/4 tbsp cornstarch

- 1/4 cup of chicken broth (preferably low-sodium)

- 1 1/2 tbsp honey

- 2 cloves of garlic (minced)

- 1/4 cup of soy sauce (preferably low-sodium)

Ingredients for the stir-fry:

- 1 cup of broccoli florets

- 1 tbsp oil

- 1/2 cup of carrots (peeled, sliced thinly)

- 1/2 lb chicken thighs (boneless, skinless, cut into small pieces)

- 1/2 cup snow peas

- 1 bell pepper (stem and seeds removed, sliced thinly)

- 1/2 cup of water chestnuts (sliced)

- 1 clove of garlic

- salt

- pepper

- 3 cups of quinoa (cooked, for serving)

Directions:

1. In a bowl, add all of the sauce ingredients, then whisk until well combined. Set aside.

2. In another bowl, add the chicken with salt and pepper, then toss to season.

3. In a skillet, add half of the oil over medium-high heat.

4. When the oil is hot, add the chicken and stir-fry for about 4 to 5 minutes until the cubes are completely cooked through.

5. Transfer the chicken to a plate.

6. Add the rest of the oil to the same skillet.

7. When the oil is hot, add the pepper, carrots, broccoli, garlic, carrots, and snow peas, then stir-fry for about 5 minutes.

8. Add the chicken back to the skillet along with the sauce.

9. Stir-fry everything together, then allow it to cook for about 1 to 2 minutes undisturbed for the sauce to thicken.

10. Divide the quinoa between 3 plates and top with the stir-fried chicken and veggies.

11. Serve while hot.

Broccoli Shrimp

Beef and broccoli are popular combinations, but have you ever tried beef and shrimp? This is a flavorful and vibrant dish that you can make with your child to introduce them to the process of stir-frying.

Time: *20 minutes*

Serving Size: *2 servings*

Prep Time: *5 minutes*

Cook Time: *15 minutes*

Ingredients:

- 1/2 tbsp cornstarch

- 1/2 tsp honey

- 1 tbsp rice vinegar

- 1/8 cup of soy sauce (low sodium)

- 1 1/2 tbsp vegetable oil (divided)

- 2 cups of white rice (cooked)

- 1 cup of broccoli florets

- 2 cloves of garlic (minced)

- 1/2 lb shrimp (peeled, deveined)

- salt

- pepper

Directions:

1. In a bowl, add the shrimp and cornstarch, then toss to coat. Set aside.

2. In a skillet, add half of the oil over high heat.

3. When the oil is hot, add the shrimp, salt, and pepper, then stir-fry for about 4 minutes.

4. Transfer the cooked shrimp to a plate.

5. Add the rest of the oil to the same skillet along with the garlic, and stir-fry for about 30 seconds.

6. Add the broccoli and stir-fry for about 2 minutes.

7. Add the shrimp back into the skillet along with the rice vinegar, honey, and soy sauce. Stir everything well and bring the mixture to a boil.

8. Allow to boil for about 1 to 2 minutes until the broccoli is fork-tender and the shrimp has become opaque.

9. Serve while hot with rice.

Simple Sesame Tofu

Stir-frying different ingredients will give your child the confidence to perform this cooking method. In this recipe, you will be using tofu, a plant-based protein that cooks quickly, so you need to be mindful!

Time: *25 minutes*

Serving Size: *3 servings*

Prep Time: *20 minutes*

Cook Time: *5 minutes*

Ingredients:

- 1/4 tsp fine salt

- 1 tsp canola oil (divided)

- 1/2 tbsp sesame oil

- 1 tbsp soy sauce

- 3 tbsp lime juice (freshly squeezed)

- 1 block of tofu (firm, pressed to remove excess water, cut into cubes)

- sesame seeds (for garnish)

Directions:

1. In a bowl, add the sesame oil, lime juice, and soy sauce, then mix well.

2. Add the tofu cubes and toss to coat.

3. Allow the tofu to marinate for about 10 minutes.

4. Drain and discard the marinade.

5. In a pan, add half of the canola oil over medium heat.

6. When the oil is hot, add the tofu, then stir-fry for about 4 to 5 minutes

7. After cooking, transfer the tofu to a bowl.

8. Top with sesame seeds and serve immediately.

Sticky Pork

This stir-fried dish is super simple yet packed with flavor. If you allow your child to handle the raw ingredients, remember to wash their hands. Then, you can have fun while cooking this dish.

Time: *30 minutes*

Serving Size: *2 servings*

Prep Time: *20 minutes*

Cook Time: *10 minutes*

Ingredients:

- 1 tsp sesame oil

- 1/2 tsp Chinese five-spice powder

- 1 tbsp ketchup

- 1 tbsp honey

- 1 tbsp soy sauce

- 2 cups of egg noodles (cooked)

- 1 pork tenderloin (cut into small pieces)

- 1 cup of your child's favorite veggies (peeled, chopped)

Directions:

1. In a bowl, add the ketchup, honey, five spice powder, and soy sauce, then mix well.

2. Add the pork and toss well to coat the pieces.

3. In a pan, add the oil over medium heat.

4. When the oil is hot, add the pork with its sauce, then stir-fry for about 4 to 5 minutes until the pieces of pork start to brown.

5. Add the vegetables, and stir-fry for about 2 to 3 minutes.

6. Add the egg noodles, and stir-fry for about 1 to 2 minutes.

7. Serve while hot.

Chicken, Veggies, and Noodles

The great thing about stir-fried dishes is that you can use different ingredients for them! Here is a recipe with chicken, veggies, and some noodles. It's tasty. Nutritious, and satisfying with each bite.

Time: 10 *minutes (marinating time not included)*

Serving Size: 2 *servings*

Prep Time: 10 *minutes*

Cook Time: 20 *minutes*

Ingredients for the chicken:

- 1/2 tsp ginger (fresh, grated)

- 1/2 tbsp Honey

- 1 tbsp soy sauce

- 1 chicken thigh (skinless, boneless)

- 1 clove of garlic (crushed)

Other ingredients:

- 1/4 tsp honey

- 1/4 tsp mirin

- 1/4 tbsp sunflower oil

- 1/4 cup of broccoli florets

- 1/4 cup of chicken stock

- 2/3 cups of egg noodles (preferably whole wheat)

- 1/2 red pepper (stem and seeds removed, chopped)

- 1 small carrot (peeled, grated)

Directions:

1. In a bowl, add all of the marinade ingredients except for the chicken and mix well.

2. Add the chicken to the bowl and toss to coat the small pieces/

3. Allow the chicken to marinate for about 1 hour.

4. After marinating, add the sunflower oil to a pan over medium heat.

5. When the oil is hot, add the chicken along with the marinade, then stir-fry for about 10 minutes.

6. Add the pepper, broccoli, carrots, and chicken stock. Mix well and allow to simmer until the sauce thickens.

7. Add the noodles and stir-fry until everything is well combined.

8. Divide the stir-fried meal between 2 bowls and serve while hot.

Chapter 8:

Cooking for Special Occasions

We all love celebrating with family and friends whenever special occasions come along. Impress your guests by cooking these dishes with them. Don't forget to tell everyone how your child helped prepare the dishes so that they will feel more confident and motivated to keep cooking with you!

Birthday Cake Decorating Extravaganza

White Confetti Cake

This cake is white on the outside and bursting with colors on the inside. It's a lovely surprise for your child when you cut into the cake and hand them a slice. The best part is the cake is very tasty too!

Time: *50 minutes*

Serving Size: *8 servings*

Prep Time: *15 minutes*

Cook Time: *35 minutes*

Ingredients:

- 1 tsp vanilla extract

- 1/4 tsp fine salt

- 1/2 tbsp baking powder

- 3/4 cups of whole milk

- 1/4 cup of rainbow sprinkles

- 1 cup of sugar

- 1 stick of unsalted butter (softened)

- 1 1/2 cups of all-purpose flour

- 2 large eggs

- white frosting (vanilla flavored, homemade or store-bought)cooking spray

Directions:

1. Preheat your oven to 350°F and use cooking spray to lightly grease a cake pan, then use a sheet of parchment to line the cake pan with some excess paper hanging over the sides.

2. In a bowl, add the eggs, vanilla extract, and butter, then whisk to combine.

3. In the bowl of a stand mixed, add the sugar, flour, salt, and baking powder, then use low speed to blend until all of the ingredients are well combined.

4. Slowly add half of the liquid mixture into the bowl while continuing to beat for about 3 minutes until you get a crumbly texture.

5. Increase the speed setting to medium and continue to beat the mixture for about 1 minute until it turns fluffy.

6. Slowly add the rest of the liquid mixture while continuing to beat for about 30 seconds.

7. Add the sprinkles to the bowl and use a spatula to gently incorporate them.

8. Pour the cake batter into the pan, then use your hands to tap the rim gently. This releases any air bubbles in the batter.

9. Place the cake pan in the oven and bake the cake for about 30 to 35 minutes.

10. After baking, take the cake pan out of the oven.

11. Grasp the excess paper on the sides, gently pull the cake out of the cake pan, and gently transfer it to a wire rack to cool down completely.

12. When the cake has cooled down, spread frosting all over it until it is completely covered.

13. Slice and serve!

Fruity Cake

Adding fruits to a cake will make it more colorful and attractive to your child's eyes. It's also a great way to encourage your child to eat more fruits. Here's a recipe for a colorful cake that tastes as good as it looks.

Time: 15 minutes (chilling time not included)

Serving Size: 8 servings

Prep Time: *15 minutes*

Cook Time: *no cooking time*

Ingredients:

- 1/2 tsp vanilla extract

- 1 tbsp maple syrup

- 2/3 cup of cream

- 1 cup of mixed fresh fruit (peeled, sliced, chopped, depending on the fruits)

- 1 square cake (good for 8 people)

Directions:

1. In a bowl, add the cream, maple syrup, and vanilla extract, then mix well.

2. Spoon the whipped cream into a piping bag.

3. Pipe the whipped cream all over the surface of the cake decoratively, then top with colorful fruits.

4. Place the cake in the refrigerator to chill until ready to serve.

5. After chilling, take the cake out of the refrigerator.

6. Serve chilled.

Cookies and Cream Cake

Cookies and cream is a popular flavor among kids, and for good reason! The combination of cream and cookies is just perfect. So why not make your own cookies and cream cake with your child for both of you to enjoy?

Time: 1 *hour*

Serving Size: 8 *servings*

Prep Time: 10 *minutes*

Cook Time: 50 *minutes*

Ingredients for the cake:

- 2 tsp baking powder

- 1 tsp bicarbonate of soda

- 2 tsp vanilla extract

- 1/2 cup of strong coffee

- 1/2 cup of cocoa powder

- 1 cup of all-purpose flour

- 2/3 cup of vegetable oil

- 1 cup of buttermilk

- 2 large eggs

- 1 1/2 cups of soft, light brown sugar

- cooking spray

- a pinch of salt

Ingredients for the icing:

- 1 tsp vanilla extract

- 1/2 cup of butter (slightly salted, softened)

- 1 cup of cream cheese (full-fat)

- 1 1/4 cups of icing sugar

- 6 chocolate biscuits with vanilla cream filling (divided)

Directions:

1. Preheat your oven to 320°F, use cooking spray to lightly grease 2 baking dishes, then use a sheet of parchment to line the baking dishes with some excess paper hanging over the sides.

2. In a bowl, add the cocoa powder, flour, bicarbonate of soda, baking powder, sugar, and salt, then mix well.

3. In another bowl, add the coffee, oil, vanilla extract, eggs, and buttermilk, then whisk well.

4. Slowly pour the mixture into the bowl with the dry mixture, then whisk until well combined.

5. Divide the batter evenly between the 2 baking sheets.

6. Place the baking sheets in the oven and bake the cakes for about 25-30 minutes.

7. After baking, take the baking sheets out of the oven.

8. Grasp the excess paper on the sides, gently pull the cakes out of the baking sheets, and gently transfer them to a wire rack to cool down completely.

9. When the cakes have cooled down, prepare the icing. In a bowl, add the butter, then add half of the icing sugar by pouring it in through a strainer.

10. Use a spatula to roughly mash the ingredients together, then use a mixer to blend until you get a smooth texture.

11. Add the cream cheese and the rest of the icing sugar by pouring it through a strainer.

12. Use a spatula to roughly mash the ingredients together again, then use a mixer to blend until you get a smooth texture.

13. In a food processor, add half of the biscuits. Process until you get fine crumbs.

14. Add the cookie crumbs to the bowl of icing and mix well.

15. Spoon the icing into a piping bag.

16. Pipe some icing on top of one of the cakes and use a spatula to spread the icing all over the surface of the cake.

17. Carefully place the other cake on top of the one with the icing.

18. Use the rest of the icing to cover both layers of the cake, then pipe some icing on top decoratively.

19. Decorate the top of the cake with the rest of the biscuits.

20. Enjoy!

Triple Choco Ice Cream Cake

Who doesn't love a good slice of chocolate cake? This decadent cake is made with chocolate and ice cream, an amazing combination that's both refreshing and satisfying. It's a great cake for the whole family!

Time: *45 minutes (chilling and freezing times not included)*

Serving Size: *8 servings*

Prep Time: *20 minutes*

Cook Time: *25 minutes*

Ingredients for the cake:

- 3/4 tsp kosher salt

- 3/4 tsp baking powder

- 1 1/2 tsp baking soda

- 1 tsp vanilla extract

- 3 tbsp safflower oil

- 3/4 cup of cocoa powder (unsweetened)

- 3/4 cup of buttermilk

- 3/4 cup of water (warm)

- 1 1/2 cups of sugar

- 1 1/2 cups of all-purpose flour

- 2 large eggs

- cooking spray

Ingredients for the ganache:

- 1 cup of heavy cream

- 1 1/2 cups of white chocolate (chopped)

Ingredients for the filling:

- 2 pints of ice cream (chocolate flavored, softened)

- milk chocolate shavings (for serving)

- whipped cream (lightly sweetened, for serving)

Directions:

1. Preheat your oven to 350°F; use cooking spray to lightly grease 2 cake pans, then use a sheet of parchment to line the cake pans with some excess paper hanging over the sides.

2. In the bowl of an electric mixer, add the flour, cocoa, sugar, baking powder, baking soda, and salt, then use low speed to

beat everything together until all of the ingredients are just combined.

3. Add the oil, vanilla extract, buttermilk, and eggs, then continue to beat until well combined.

4. Turn the mixer up to medium speed, add the water, and beat for about 3 minutes until you get a smooth batter.

5. Divide the cake batter evenly between 2 cake pans.

6. Place the cake pans in the oven and bake the cakes for about 12 to 15 minutes.

7. After baking, take the cake pans out of the oven.

8. Grasp the excess paper on the sides, gently pull the cakes out of the cake pans, and gently transfer them to a wire rack to cool down completely.

9. When the cakes have cooled down, take the bowl of ganache out of the refrigerator.

10. Spread a thick layer of ice cream all over the surface of one of the cakes, then place the other cake on top of it.

11. Use a sheet of cling wrap to cover the whole cake, then place it in the freezer overnight.

12. About an hour before serving, prepare the ganache. In a saucepan, add the cream and heat it on the stove over medium heat.

13. Pour the hot cream into a bowl with the white chocolate, then allow to sit for about 3 minutes.

14. Use a spatula to gently mix the cream and chocolate until both ingredients are fully combined.

15. Cover the bowl and place it in the refrigerator for about 1 hour to chill.

16. After freezing, take the cake out of the freezer, and take the bowl of ganache out of the refrigerator.

17. Unwrap the cake and spread the ganache all over it.

18. Decorate the cake with whipped cream and chocolate shavings.

19. Slice and serve immediately.

Rainbow Cereal Cake

Decorating a cake with rainbow-colored cereal is a fun way to make a colorful cake with different textures. While you may use your child's favorite cereal for this cake, Fruit Loops are the perfect choice.

Time: *1 hour, 5 minutes*

Serving Size: *8 servings*

Prep Time: *20 minutes*

Cook Time: *45 minutes*

Ingredients:

- 1/2 cup of vegetable oil

- 1 cup of milk

- 2 cups of Fruit Loops cereal

- 1 bag of cake mix (enough to serve 8 people)

- 3 eggs

- cooking spray

- white frosting (homemade or store-bought)

Directions:

1. In a bowl, add the milk and half of the cereal.

2. Mix well and set aside for the milk to absorb the flavor of the cereal.

3. Preheat your oven to 325°F; use cooking spray to lightly grease a cake pan, then use a sheet of parchment to line the cake pan with some excess paper hanging over the sides.

4. In a bowl, add the oil, eggs, and the cake mix, then whisk until everything is well combined.

5. Pour the milk into the bowl through a strainer so the cereal gets left behind, then mix everything well.

6. Pour the cake batter into the cake pan.

7. Place the cake pan in the oven and bake the cake for about 40 to 45 minutes.

8. After baking, take the cake pans out of the oven.

9. Grasp the excess paper on the sides, gently pull the cakes out of the cake pan, and gently transfer it to a wire rack to cool down completely.

10. When the cake has cooled down, use a spatula to spread white frosting all over it.

11. Decorate the cake with the rest of the Fruit Loops cereal.

12. Slice and serve!

Holiday-Themed Treats

Choco-Coated Ice Cream Sweet Hearts

Valentine's Day is the day we celebrate all kinds of love. Whipping up a sweet treat for your whole family is a nice way to show them how much you care. This simple recipe is a lot of fun to make!

Time: *20 minutes (freezing time not included)*

Serving Size: *2 servings*

Prep Time: *20 minutes*

Cook Time: *no cooking time*

Ingredients:

- 3 tbsp coconut oil

- 1/4 cup of candy melts (pink or white)

- 3/4 cup of chocolate (chopped)

- 1 pint of ice cream (strawberry flavored or any other flavor)

Directions:

1. Lay the pint of ice cream on its side, then use a sharp knife to cut it into thick slices.

2. Use a heart-shaped cookie cutter to cut out heart shapes from the ice cream slices, then place them on a baking sheet.

3. Place the baking sheet in the freezer and freeze the hearts for about 30 minutes.

4. Right before taking the hearts out, prepare the coating. In a microwave-safe bowl, add the chocolate and coconut oil.

5. Place the bowl in the microwave and heat on high for about 30 seconds.

6. Take the bowl out and stir the ingredients together. Keep doing this until all of the chocolate has melted and has completely been mixed with the coconut oil.

7. Repeat the same melting steps for the candy melts.

8. Take the baking sheet out of the freezer and prepare a wire rack. Place a plate under the wire rack to catch the chocolate drippings.

9. Dip one of the ice cream hearts in the melted chocolate, then place it on the wire rack. Do the same for the rest of the ice cream hearts.

10. Drizzle melted candy melts decoratively on top of the coated ice cream hearts.

11. Place the wire rack in the freezer for a minimum of 15 minutes for the chocolate to harden.

12. Serve chilled.

Easter Bunny Biscuits

These biscuits are colorful, cute, and the perfect treat for any Easter celebration. Make a whole experience for your child by asking them to help you make these tasty bunny biscuits and then serving them to the whole family.

Time: *20 minutes (chilling time not included)*

Serving Size: *5 servings*

Prep Time: *20 minutes*

Cook Time: *no cooking time*

Ingredients:

- 1/3 cup of rainbow sprinkles

- 2/3 cup of milk chocolate (chopped, then melted)

- 2/3 cup of white chocolate (chopped, then melted)

- 15 jumbo marshmallows (sliced in half diagonally)

- 15 oval-shaped biscuits

Directions:

1. Use baking paper to line a big baking tray, then place the biscuits on the tray.

2. Spread melted chocolate all over the biscuits. You may use either milk chocolate or white chocolate, then top with rainbow sprinkles.

3. Dip the pointed tip of the marshmallow halves in chocolate, then stick 2 each at the tip of each biscuit to make the ears.

4. Place the baking tray in the refrigerator for about 15 minutes for the chocolate to set.

5. Enjoy after chilling.

Spooky Halloween Bark

When Halloween comes along, all types of sweets come out along with those spooky creatures. Add to the fun of the holiday by making your own spooky and colorful chocolate bark. Add anything you want to it!

Time: *15 minutes (chilling time not included)*

Serving Size: *4 servings*

Prep Time: *15 minutes*

Cook Time: *no cooking time*

Ingredients:

- 1 tsp food coloring (orange)

- 1 tsp food coloring (black)

- 1/8 cup of edible eyes

- 1/2 cup of yellow, brown, and orange-colored sweets

- 1/2 cup of dark chocolate (chopped, then melted)

- 1 cup of white chocolate (chopped, then melted)

Directions:

1. Use a sheet of parchment paper to line a big baking tray.

2. Add the orange food coloring to the melted white chocolate and mix to combine.

3. Add the black food coloring to the melted dark chocolate and mix to combine.

4. Pour the colored chocolates into the baking tray, then use a toothpick to swirl the colors around.

5. Scatter the sweets all over the melted chocolate.

6. Decorate the bark with the edible eyes by placing them all over.

7. Place the baking tray in the refrigerator for at least 20 minutes for the chocolate to harden.

8. After chilling, take the baking tray out and break the bark into pieces

9. Serve on a spooky-colored plate.

Turkey Centerpiece

A roasted turkey is the most anticipated centerpiece on any Thanksgiving table. Here, you will be making a different type of turkey as it will be made of a ball of cheese. This is another fun dish for you and your child to have fun making together.

Time: 25 minutes (chilling time not included)

Serving Size: 6 servings

Prep Time: 25 minutes

Cook Time: no cooking time

Ingredients:

- 1/2 cup of mixed nuts (chopped)

- 1/8 cup of chocolate (chopped, then melted)

- 1 cup of cheddar cheese (shredded)

- 1 candy corn

- 1 cup of cream cheese (softened)

- 1 pack of round crackers

- 1 round chocolate candy (for the turkey's head)

- 2 edible eyes

- 1 Slim Jim

- a handful of pretzel sticks

Directions:

1. In a food processor, add the cream cheese and blend until you get a smooth texture.

2. Add the cheddar cheese and continue to blend until both cheeses are thoroughly combined.

3. Spoon the mixture into a clean surface and roll it into a big cheese ball.

4. Use a sheet of cling wrap to cover the cheese ball completely.

5. Place the cheese ball in the refrigerator for a minimum of 2 hours to firm up.

6. When the cheese ball has firmed up, take it out of the refrigerator and unwrap it.

7. Add the chopped nuts to a shallow dish, then roll the cheese ball around it to coat it with nuts completely.

8. Place the cheese ball on a plate, then stick the pretzel sticks in one line behind the cheese ball to make the turkey's tail.

9. Slice off the end of the Slim Jim, then spread some melted chocolate on the tip.

10. Stick the round chocolate ball at the end of the Slim Jim to make the head of the turkey.

11. Gently push the other end of the Slim Jim into the cheese ball to attach it to the body.

12. Spread some melted chocolate at the back of the edible eyes, then stick them on the round chocolate ball.

13. Spread some melted chocolate on the back of the candy corn and stick it on the chocolate ball as well to make the beak.

14. Arrange the round crackers around the cheese ball so that it looks like the turkey is sitting on a nest of crackers.

15. Place it in the center of the table and enjoy!

Do You Want to Build a Snowman Cupcake?

It's always fun to bake cupcakes with your child. And it's even more fun to decorate those cupcakes after baking them. When Christmastime comes along, ask your child if they want to build a snowman cupcake with you and watch their face light up.

Time: 50 *minutes*

Serving Size: 12 *servings*

Prep Time: 20 *minutes*

Cook Time: 30 *minutes*

Ingredients for the cupcakes:

- 1 1/2 tsp baking powder

- 1/2 tsp bicarbonate of soda

- 2 tbsp sour cream

- 1/3 cup of sunflower oil

- 1/4 cup of cocoa powder

- 1/2 cup of water (boiling)

- 1 cup of caster sugar

- 3/4 cup of all-purpose flour

- 2 large eggs

- a pinch of salt

Ingredients for the icing:

- 2 tbsp milk

- 1 cup of butter (unsalted, softened)

- 2 cups of icing sugar

Ingredients for the decorations:

- 2 tsp coconut (desiccated)

- 1 cup of fondant icing (white)

- black icing

- food coloring paste (orange)

- food coloring paste (red)

- 12 pretzel sticks (broken in half)

- 12 white marshmallows

Directions:

1. Preheat your oven to 320°F and line the cups of a muffin tin with decorative cupcake liners.

2. In a bowl, sift the cocoa, flour, sugar, bicarbonate of soda, baking powder, and salt, then mix well.

3. Add the eggs, sour cream, and sunflower oil, then mix well until you get a smooth batter.

4. Add the boiling water, then mix again until the batter is silky smooth.

5. Pour the batter into the cupcake liners making sure not to fill each muffin cup. Also, try to add the same amount of batter into each muffin cup so that they all cook evenly.

6. Place the muffin tin in the oven and bake the cupcakes for about 20 to 22 minutes.

7. After baking, take the muffin tin out of the oven and allow the cupcakes to cool down for about 5 minutes.

8. Transfer the cupcakes to a wire rack and allow them to cool down completely.

9. When the cupcakes have cooled down, prepare the icing. In a bowl, add the butter and beat until you get a light and pale texture.

10. Slowly add the milk and icing sugar while beating until you get a smooth texture.

11. Spoon the icing into a piping bag.

12. Take a small portion of fondant icing and add the orange food coloring to it.

13. Mix well until the fondant turns orange.

14. Take small portions of the orange fondant and roll each portion into a small carrot nose.

15. Take a bigger portion of fondant icing and add the red food coloring to it.

16. Mix well until the fondant turns red.

17. Take small portions of the red fondant and roll each out into a long strip for the snowman's scarf.

18. Spoon the black icing into a piping bag with a very fine tip, then use the icing to draw eyes and a mouth on each of the marshmallows.

19. Add some icing to the flat part of the fondant carrots, then stick them on the marshmallows as well.

20. Pipe a dollop of icing onto a cupcake, then top with a decorated marshmallow.

21. Twist the scarf below the marshmallow, then stick one pretzel stick on each side for the arms.

22. Pipe small dots on the icing to make the snowman buttons.

23. Take a photo and serve!

Cooking for Family Celebrations

Valentine Family Hugs

Hugs are warm and sweet, which is why we all love them. Aside from hugging your child, try making these sweet hugs with them too. Each treat is like a sweet little hug that will bring a smile to anyone's face.

Time: 10 *minutes*

Serving Size: 4 *servings*

Prep Time: 6 *minutes*

Cook Time: 4 *minutes*

Ingredients:

- 12 kisses chocolates

- 12 M&Ms (pink or red)

- 12 pretzels (square-shaped)

- rainbow sprinkles

Directions:

1. Preheat your oven to 320°F and use a sheet of parchment to line a baking sheet.

2. Place the pretzels on the baking sheet, then place 1 chocolate kiss on top of each pretzel.

3. Place the baking sheet in the oven and bake the pretzels for about 4 minutes until the kisses have softened.

4. After baking, take the baking sheet out of the oven.

5. Top each kiss with an M&M, then gently press down for all of the ingredients to stick together.

6. Top with rainbow sprinkles.

7. Allow the hugs to cool down completely before serving.

Easter Chocolate Nest

When Easter comes along, all we can see are bunnies, eggs, and chicks! Make this fun Easter treat to serve to your whole family for your next gathering. It's super easy to bring together, and it will surely make all of your guests smile.

Time: 10 *minutes (chilling time not included)*

Serving Size: 6 *servings*

Prep Time: 10 *minutes*

Cook Time: *no cooking time*

Ingredients:

- 1/2 cup of butter (unsalted)

- 4 tbsp golden syrup

- 1 cup of dark chocolate

- 3/4 cup of cornflakes

- 1 1/2 cups of mixed chocolate Easter eggs

- water (to help melt the chocolate)

Directions:

1. Fill a pot with water, then place it over medium heat.

2. Bring the water to a boil, then turn the heat down to allow the water to simmer gently.

3. In a bowl, add the butter, chocolate, and syrup.

4. Place the bowl over the pot of water and stir everything together until the chocolate melts and all of the ingredients are well combined.

5. Add the cornflakes and mix well until the cornflakes are completely coated with the chocolate mixture.

6. Transfer the mixture into a bundt tin, spread it around, and press down so the mixture follows the shape of the tin.

7. Place the bundt tin in the refrigerator for about 2 hours for the chocolate nest to harden.

8. After chilling, take the bundt tin out of the refrigerator.

9. Gently tip the bundt tin over and shake it gently until the chocolate nest comes out.

10. Pour the chocolate eggs into the middle of the nest.

11. Serve immediately.

Spooky Mac and Cheese Bowls

If you're planning a Halloween party, you need to have a lot of spooky food. For this recipe, you will carve some bell peppers instead of pumpkins to make mini Jack-O-Lanterns filled with mac and cheese.

Time: *40 minutes*

Serving Size: *6 servings*

Prep Time: *20 minutes*

Cook Time: *20 minutes*

Ingredients:

- 1 cup of cream cheese (softened)

- 1 cup of elbow macaroni (uncooked)

- 1 1/4 cups of half-and-half

- 1 1/2 cup of mild cheddar cheese (shredded)

- 6 orange bell peppers (top part cut off to remove the seeds inside)

- kosher salt

- water (for cooking the macaroni)

Directions:

1. Fill a pot with water and a pinch of salt, then place it over medium heat. Bring to a boil.

2. When the water is boiling, add the bell peppers along with the tops.

3. Cook for about 2 to 3 minutes, then use a slotted spoon to take them out of the water. Set aside to cool down.

4. Bring the water to a boil once again, then add the macaroni. Cook for about 6 minutes until the macaroni is just tender.

5. Drain the water and reserve 1 cup of the cooking liquid. Set the noodles and liquid aside.

6. In a saucepan, add the half and half over medium heat, then bring to a simmer.

7. Allow to simmer for about 10 minutes, then add the cream cheese. Stir well until the cheese is fully combined with the half and half.

8. Add the cheddar cheese and mix well until you form a smooth sauce.

9. Add the macaroni and a pinch of salt to the saucepan, then mix well.

10. Use a sharp knife to carve faces into the cooked bell peppers, then fill them with mac and cheese.

11. Complete the look by placing the top of the bell peppers to cover them.

12. Serve immediately.

Healthy Thanksgiving Turkey

There is nothing more traditional than a roasted turkey during Thanksgiving. For something fun, colorful, and healthy, create a different version of a turkey by using a combination of tasty ingredients. Here's how!

Time: *15 minutes*

Serving Size: *4 servings*

Prep Time: *15 minutes*

Cook Time: *no cooking time*

Ingredients:

- 1 baby carrot

- 1 pear (cut in half lengthwise, seeds removed)

- 1 red bell pepper (stems and seeds removed, sliced)

- 1 slice of pepperoni

- 1 yellow bell pepper (stems and seeds removed, sliced)

- 2 edible eyes

- peanut butter

Directions:

1. Lay down the pear on a plate with the sliced side facing down.

2. Spread some peanut butter at the back of the edible eyes and stick them on the narrow part of the pear.

3. Cut 2 slices from the baby carrot and carve the slices to look like the turkey's legs.

4. Cut 2 slices from the baby carrot and carve the slices to look like the turkey's feet.

5. Cut another slice from the baby carrot and carve it to look like the beak.

6. Spread some peanut butter on 1 side of the carrot beak, then stick it on the face.

7. Cut the crown of the turkey from the slice of pepperoni, then use peanut butter to stick it on top of the turkey's head.

8. Arrange the bell pepper slices on both sides of the turkey to make the feathers.

9. Serve and enjoy!

Snowy and Creamy Log

This beautiful treat looks just like a log left outside in the snow. When you slice it open, you will see the lovely and tasty layers that you and your child have created together. It's an impressive dessert that's quite easy to make.

Time: *20 minutes (chilling time not included)*

Serving Size: *8 servings*

Prep Time: *20 minutes*

Cook Time: *no cooking time*

Ingredients:

- 3 tbsp lemon juice (freshly squeezed)

- 1 tbsp lemon zest

- ¼ cup of milk

- 1/2 cup of cream cheese

- 1/2 cup of condensed milk

- 2 cups of butter biscuits

- 3/4 cup of cream

- chocolate (grated, for topping)

Directions:

1. In the bowl of a mixer, add the lemon rind and cream cheese, then beat until you get a soft and creamy texture.

2. Add the lemon juice and condensed milk, then continue to beat until all of the ingredients are completely combined.

3. Transfer the cream into a bowl, then place in the refrigerator for a minimum of 2 hours for the cream to thicken.

4. After chilling, continue with the steps. Take the bowl with the cream out of the refrigerator.

5. In another bowl, add the milk.

6. Dip one of the biscuits into the milk.

7. Spread the cream on one side of another biscuit, then put it together with the biscuit dipped in milk to form a biscuit sandwich.

8. Place the biscuit sandwich on a plate.

9. Repeat the biscuit sandwich-making steps until you have used up all of the biscuits. Arrange the biscuits on the plate to look like a log.

10. Place the plate in the refrigerator for about 15 to 20 minutes to chill the biscuit sandwiches and make them firm.

11. After chilling, take the plate out of the refrigerator.

12. In a bowl, add the cream and beat until you can form soft peaks.

13. Spread the cream decoratively all over the biscuit sandwich log, then top with grated chocolate.

14. Place the plate back in the refrigerator to chill for a minimum of 2 hours.

15. Slice and serve after chilling.

Chapter 9:

Kitchen Science and Fun

Did you know that you can make cooking even more fun by presenting it in creative ways? Here are some fun recipes for you to do with your child that will surely make them love and appreciate the art of cooking.

Food Experiments

Magic Minute Cake

Have you ever tried baking a cake in just a matter of minutes? This is one experiment that will surely excite your child, especially if they're craving cakes when it's not their birthday!

Time: *3 minutes*

Serving Size: *1 serving*

Prep Time: *2 minutes*

Cook Time: *1 minute*

Ingredients:

- 1 tsp vanilla extract

- 1/4 tsp baking powder

- 2 tsp butter (melted)

- 2 tbsp cocoa powder

- 1 tbsp milk

- 1/4 cup of flour

- 2 tbsp white sugar

- 1 egg

Directions:

1. In a microwave-safe mug, add the butter, then swirl it around to coat the insides of the mug.

2. Add the rest of the ingredients to the mug, then use a fork to whisk everything together until you form a smooth cake batter.

3. Place the mug in the microwave and heat it up for 1 minute.

4. Take the mug out and check if the cake is done. Ideally, it would already be completely baked for your child to be delighted. If not, you may put the mug back in the microwave and heat up the mug cake in 5-second intervals until it's baked.

5. Serve this mug cake with a spoon!

Bagged Slushie

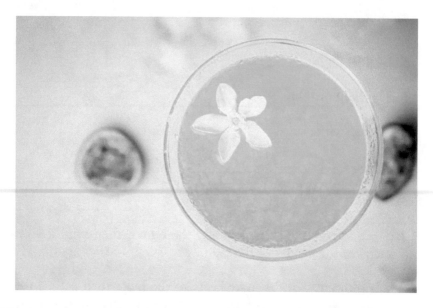

Have you ever tried making a slushie in a bag? Do you think it's even possible? Well, it is. And if your child likes to be amazed, this is one recipe you should try with them. It's easy, simple, and amazing!

Time: *10 minutes*

Serving Size: *2 servings*

Prep Time: *10 minutes*

Cook Time: *no cooking time*

Ingredients:

- 1 cup of salt

- 1 cup of water

- 2 cups of apple juice

- 2 cups of ice

- food coloring (blue and red, optional)

Directions:

1. Add half of the apple juice and a few drops of red food coloring to a quart-sized Ziploc bag, then seal the bag.

2. Add the rest of the apple juice and a few drops of blue food coloring to another quart-sized Ziploc bag, then seal the bag.

3. Add the water, ice, and salt to a gallon-sized Ziploc bag, then add the 2 smaller bags to the bag as well.

4. Vigorously shake the big bag for about 3 to 5 minutes.

5. After shaking, open the big bag and take out the smaller bags.

6. Scoop the slushies out of the smaller bags, place them in glasses, and serve!

Colorful Rock Candy

This experiment requires a lot of patience, as it takes time for the rock candies to "grow." But if you and your child can wait, you will end up with colorful, pretty, and sweet candies.

Time: *8 to 10 days*

Serving Size: *depends on how much you make*

Prep Time: *8 to 10 days*

Cook Time: *around 45 minutes*

Ingredients:

- food coloring (any color)

- sugar (granulated)

- water

Directions:

1. Pour the water into a cup, then prepare a clean plate, a jar, and some pieces of string that are about 2 inches longer than the jar's height. Also, prepare a shallow dish filled with sugar.

2. Soak the pieces of string in the water for about 5 minutes.

3. After soaking, take 1 piece of string, then use your fingers to squeeze out any excess water.

4. Place the string on the dish with sugar, then roll it around to coat the string with sugar.

5. Gently unroll the string and place it on the clean plate.

6. Repeat the same steps for all the pieces of string, then leave them to dry on the plate overnight.

7. The next day, tie one end of the strings to a small, clean object like a small screw.

8. Tie the other end of the strings to a stick that's longer than the mouth of your jar.

9. Carefully place the stick on top of the jar to see if the strings aren't too short or too long. Adjust the length of the strings so that each of them is hanging around 1/3-inch from the bottom of the jar.

10. After adjusting the lengths of the strings, set them aside.

11. In a pot, add some water over medium heat. Bring to a boil.

12. When the water is boiling, carefully pour the hot water into the jar.

13. In the same pot, add 1/2 cup of water over low heat.

14. Add 1 cup of sugar, then use a wooden spoon to stir the mixture until the sugar dissolves completely.

15. Turn the heat up to medium and bring the mixture to a boil.

16. Take the pot off the heat, then add 1 tablespoon of sugar at a time.

17. Each time you add sugar, stir the mixture until all of the sugar dissolves completely. Keep doing this until you cannot dissolve any more sugar. You may add some food coloring, too, to make your rock crystals colored.

18. Allow the mixture to cool down for about 5 minutes.

19. After 5 minutes, carefully pour out the water from the jar, then replace it with the sugar mixture.

20. Carefully place the stick on the rim of the jar and drop the weighted strings inside.

21. Use a paper towel to loosely cover the jar so that it won't get contaminated.

22. Leave the jar for about 1 week without being disturbed. Each day, you can check the growth of the rock crystals. Just make sure not to move the jar while you do so.

23. After about 1 week, gently pull out the stick with all of the strings attached to it. You will see the rock candies attached to the strings.

24. Rinse the rock candies with cold water, then place them on a paper towel to dry for about 30 minutes.

25. When the rock candies are dry, enjoy!

Fluffy and Soft Cloud Bread

After making some hard rock candies, it's time to make something soft, fluffy, and tasty. Here is a recipe for cloud bread that you and your child can make at home. The best part would be eating the soft, pillowy bread when it's done.

Time: *35 minutes*

Serving Size: *2 servings*

Prep Time: *15 minutes*

Cook Time: *20 minutes*

Ingredients:

- 1/2 tsp vanilla extract

- 1 tbsp cornstarch

- 2 1/2 tbsp confectioner's sugar

- 3 eggs (whites only)

Directions:

1. Preheat your oven to 300°F and use a sheet of parchment to line a baking sheet.

2. In the bowl of a mixer, add the egg whites and vanilla extract, then beat until the egg whites turn frothy.

3. Slowly add the cornstarch and sugar while beating until you can form stiff peaks.

4. Scoop the cloud bread batter onto the baking sheet and use a spatula to create any shape you would like for the bread.

5. Place the baking sheet in the oven and bake the cloud bread for about 20 minutes.

6. After baking, take the baking sheet out of the oven.

7. Allow the cloud bread to cool down before serving.

Mallow Slime

Does your child love to play with slime? If so, here is a fun experiment that's totally edible. Make sure to supervise your child for this, as you will be heating up the marshmallows as part of the process.

Time: *5 minutes*

Serving Size: *1 serving*

Prep Time: *5 minutes*

Cook Time: *no cooking time*

Ingredients:

- 1 tbsp cooking oil

- 1 tbsp cornstarch

- 6 jumbo marshmallows

Directions:

1. In a microwave-safe bowl, add the marshmallows, then drizzle the oil over them.

2. Place the bowl in the microwave, then heat the marshmallows and oil for about 30 seconds on high.

3. Take the bowl out of the microwave, add the cornstarch, and mix well.

4. Continue to mix the marshmallow slime until it cools down.

5. When it's cool enough to handle, you can serve it to your child so they can play and eat as they wish!

Edible Art Projects

Rainbow Toast

This will be the prettiest piece of bread you will make with your child. Once it's done, you can eat it on its own or use the colorful bread to make a lovely and tasty sandwich!

Time: *10 minutes*

Serving Size: *2 servings*

Prep Time: *10 minutes*

Cook Time: *no cooking time*

Ingredients:

- 1 1/2 cups of milk

- 4 slices of bread

- food coloring (red, orange, yellow, green, blue, purple)

Directions:

1. Pour the milk into 6 cups and add 2 drops of food coloring to each cup. Mix well.

2. Use clean paintbrushes to "paint" the slices of bread using the colored milk.

3. After painting, allow the slices of bread to dry up a bit.

4. Toast the slices of bread lightly.

5. Serve on their own or with your favorite spreads.

Soft and Squishy Love Bugs

Making food art is a lot of fun, especially when you can tell stories with the edible artwork you make. For example, you can use different colors to make these love bugs and then use them as puppets to tell a story!

Time: *15 minutes*

Serving Size: *2 servings*

Prep Time: *15 minutes*

Cook Time: *no cooking time*

Ingredients:

- 4 large gumdrops

- 4 mini gumdrops

- 8 spaghetti noodles (uncooked)

- 12 marshmallows

- black icing

- light syrup

- confetti sprinkles (heart-shaped)

- sprinkles (pink colored)

- sugar

- water

Directions:

1. Thread 3 marshmallows each on lollipop sticks.

2. Fill a glass with water, then dip the marshmallow skewers into it.

3. Quickly remove the marshmallow skewers from the water, then use a paper towel to gently dab off excess water.

4. Roll the marshmallow skewers in a shallow dish filled with pink sprinkles to coat them completely, then place the marshmallow skewers on a plate lined with wax paper.

5. Spoon the black icing into a small Ziploc bag, then cut off a very small portion of the tip to make a piping bag with a fine tip.

6. Spread syrup on 2 heart-shaped confetti sprinkles and stick them on the top marshmallow of each skewer to make the eyes.

7. Pipe 1 black dot of icing on each of the hearts, then pipe a curved line below the eyes to make the smile.

8. Use a knife to slice the mini gum drops in half crosswise, then insert an uncooked spaghetti noodle into the top curved half of the gum drops.

9. Insert the other end of the uncooked spaghetti noodle on the top marshmallow to create the antenna of the love bug. If the noodle is too long, just break off a piece of it.

10. Roll the large gumdrops in a shallow dish filled with sugar and coat them completely.

11. Use a rolling pin to flatten the jumbo gumdrops, then use a mini heart-shaped cookie cutter to cut out small hearts.

12. Spread syrup on one side of the small hearts, then stick them at the back of the marshmallow skewers to make the wings.

13. Allow the marshmallow skewers to sit for about 10 minutes for all of the components to set.

14. Enjoy!

Monster Sandwich

This is a fun recipe where you can ask your child to use their imagination to make their own monster. Demonstrate how to make a monster sandwich by following this recipe, then allow your child to follow along or create their own.

Time: 10 *minutes*

Serving Size: 1 *serving*

Prep Time: 10 *minutes*

Cook Time: *no cooking time*

Ingredients:

- 1 slice of cheddar cheese (sliced into small triangles)

- 2 green olives

- 2 slices of bread

- 2 slices of turkey ham

- mustard, mayonnaise, or ketchup

Directions:

1. Use a round cookie cutter to cut the bread slices into big circles.

2. Spread mustard, mayonnaise, or ketchup on 1 side of the bread slices.

3. Layer the turkey ham on one of the bread slices, then arrange the small triangles around the edge to make the monster's teeth.

4. Place the other bread on top to complete the sandwich.

5. Insert toothpicks into the olives, then insert the other end of the toothpicks into the top of the sandwich to make the eyes.

6. Growl and serve!

Baked Mr. Potato Head

Do you remember the healthy turkey you made with your child? Well, here is another fun recipe where you will create a new version of something classic. This time, you will recreate Mr. Potato Head using different ingredients.

Time: *1 hour, 30 minutes*

Serving Size: *2 servings*

Prep Time: *30 minutes*

Cook Time: *1 hour*

Ingredients:

- 1 potato

- baby corn

- beans (canned, drained, rinsed)

- bell pepper slices

- broccoli florets (steamed)

- carrot sticks and carrot slices

- cheese (shredded)

- cherry tomatoes (cut in half)

- cucumber slices

- mushroom slices

- olives (whole and sliced)

- snap peas

- spinach leaves

- olive oil

Directions:

1. Preheat your oven to 400°F.

2. Place the potato on a baking sheet.

3. Place the baking sheet in the oven and bake the potato for about 50 minutes to 1 hour until the potato is fork-tender.

4. After baking, take the baking sheet out of the oven and allow the potato to cool down.

5. Prepare all of the ingredients in shallow bowls and dishes.

6. When the potato is cool enough to handle, place it on a plate and arrange the bowls and dishes with the other ingredients around it.

7. Help your child create Mr. Potato Head using the different vegetables.

8. Serve after taking a picture of your masterpiece!

Fruity Lion Pancakes

For a fun breakfast, give this recipe a try. All you need to prepare are classic pancakes and some fruits. After making a lion, try to think about other animals you can make using pancakes too.

Time: *30 minutes*

Serving Size: *3 servings*

Prep Time: *10 minutes*

Cook Time: *20 minutes*

Ingredients for the pancakes:

- 1/2 tsp vanilla extract

- 1/4 tsp salt

- 1 1/2 tbsp sugar

- 1/2 tbsp baking powder

- 1/8 cup of butter (melted, then slightly cooled)

- 1 cup of flour

- 3/4 cup of milk

- 1 egg

- cooking spray

Ingredients for decorating the lion:

- 1 1/2 strawberries

- 3 oranges (peeled, sections separated)

- 6 raisins

- 9 chocolate-coated pretzel sticks (broken in half)

- whipped cream

Directions:

1. In a bowl, add all of the dry pancake ingredients and mix well.

2. In another bowl, add all of the wet pancake ingredients and mix well.

3. Use your finger to create a well in the center of the dry ingredient mixture.

4. Gently pour the wet ingredient mixture into the well, then mix until you form a smooth batter.

5. Allow the batter to sit for about 5 minutes while you preheat your pan, and use cooking spray to lightly grease the pan.

6. Pour the batter into the pan, then cook until you see bubbles forming on the surface.

7. Flip the pancake over and cook the other side for about 2 to 3 minutes more.

8. Transfer the cooked pancakes to a plate and allow them to cool down slightly.

9. After cooking all of the pancakes, it's time to decorate them.

10. Put a dollop of whipped cream in the middle of the pancake, then top with 1/2 piece of strawberry for the nose.

11. Arrange the pretzel sticks on both sides of the nose to make the whiskers, then place the raisins on top to make the eyes.

12. Arrange the orange segments around the pancake to make the lion's mane.

13. Take a photo with your yummy lion, then start eating!

Cooking as a Learning Experience

Tie-Dye Cake

Making this colorful cake is a wonderful learning experience for any child. Discovering how food can be made into different colors is something that any child would find fascinating. And you'll even have a tasty treat afterward.

Time: *30 minutes (chilling time not included)*

Serving Size: *6 servings*

Prep Time: *18 minutes*

Cook Time: *12 minutes*

Ingredients:

- 1 tsp baking soda

- 1/4 tsp salt

- 1 tsp vanilla extract

- 1/4 cup of butter (salted)

- 3 tbsp butter (melted)

- 1/3 cup of strawberry jam

- 2/3 cup of sugar

- 2/3 cup of cake flour

- 5 eggs (whites and yolks separated)

- 1 cup of icing sugar

- food coloring (different colors)

Directions:

1. Preheat your oven to 350°F and use a sheet of wax paper to line a baking pan.

2. Sift the baking soda, flour, and salt into a bowl, then mix them together to combine.

3. In the bowl of a mixer, add the egg yolks, then beat on high.

4. While beating, add the vanilla extract, and half of the sugar. Continue to beat until the yolks turn pale yellow and get a thicker consistency.

5. In another bowl, add the egg whites and the rest of the sugar, then whisk until you can form firm peaks.

6. Gently fold the egg yolk mixture into the bowl until both mixtures are completely incorporated.

7. Gently fold half of the dry ingredient mixture into the bowl, then do the same for the rest of the dry ingredients after a while.

8. Gently fold the melted butter into the bowl and continue mixing until you get a smooth batter.

9. Divide the batter into 6 bowls.

10. Add different colors of food coloring to each of the bowls and mix well.

11. Pour the colored cake batter into the baking pan in different patterns to create a colorful tie-dye effect.

12. Place the baking pan in the oven and bake the cake for about 10 to 12 minutes.

13. After baking, take the baking pan out of the oven.

14. Gently flip the baking pan over and shake the cake loose.

15. Peel off the wax paper, then gently roll the cake up tightly from one end to another.

16. Place the cake roll on a wire rack to cool down.

17. While the cake roll cools down, prepare the buttercream.

18. In a bowl, add the butter and beat until it turns pale yellow in color and gets a creamy consistency.

19. Slowly sift the icing sugar into the bowl, then mix to combine.

20. Add the strawberry jam and mix until well combined.

21. Gently unroll the cake and spread buttercream all over the inside, then roll it back up.

22. Place the cake roll on a plate, then place the plate in the refrigerator for about 1 hour to chill and firm up.

23. After chilling, take the cake out of the refrigerator and trim the ends off.

24. Slice and serve.

17Baked Ice Cream

Do you think you can bake ice cream without ending up with a melted puddle of goo? Your child will surely learn some new things by helping you make this clever recipe that's both amazing and delicious!

Time: *15 minutes*

Serving Size: *6 servings*

Prep Time: *11 minutes*

Cook Time: *4 minutes*

Ingredients:

- 3/4 cup of caster sugar

- 1/2 tsp cream of tartar

- 1 sponge cake (homemade or store-bought)

- ice cream (vanilla flavor)

- 3 eggs (whites only)

- jam

Directions:

1. Preheat your oven to 390°F.

2. Cut the sponge cake into 6 thick slices and arrange them on a baking sheet.

3. Spread jam all over the top of the sponge cake slices, then set aside.

4. In a bowl, add the egg whites and beat until you can form stiff peaks.

5. Slowly add the cream of tartar and half of the sugar, then whisk to combine.

6. Add the rest of the sugar, then continue whisking until you get a glossy and thick consistency.

7. Add a scoop of vanilla ice cream on each of the slices of sponge cake, then cover with a thick layer of meringue.

8. Place the baking sheet in the oven and bake the mini-baked ice cream cakes for about 3 to 4 minutes.

9. After baking, take the baking sheet out of the oven.

10. Serve immediately.

DIY Cottage Cheese

Different kinds of cheese are readily available in supermarkets and other food stores. But there is something quite amazing about the process of making your own cheese at home. Here is a simple recipe for you and your child to try out.

Time: *15 minutes*

Serving Size: *2 servings*

Prep Time: *5 minutes*

Cook Time: *10 minutes*

Ingredients:

- 1/4 cup of vinegar

- 4 cups of milk

- a pinch of salt

Directions:

1. In a saucepan, add the milk over medium heat.

2. Use a thermometer to check the temperature of the milk as you need to heat it up to 190°F.

3. When the milk reaches the right temperature, take the saucepan off the heat.

4. Add the vinegar and mix well.

5. Set the saucepan aside and allow the mixture to cool down.

6. When the cheese mixture has cooled down, pour the mixture into a bowl through a strainer.

7. The cheese will be collected by the strainer, and you can either discard or use the strained liquid for cooking.

8. Transfer the cheese to a bowl, add a pinch of salt, and mix well.

9. Serve immediately.

Colorful Dino Eggs

Make Easter a lot more interesting by making some dino eggs instead of Easter eggs. This can even be a learning activity you can have at your child's dinosaur-themed party. Either way, your child will surely be amazed while making these colorful eggs.

Time: 10 *minutes (soaking time not included)*

Serving Size: 6 *servings*

Prep Time: 10 *minutes*

Cook Time: *no cooking time*

Ingredients:

- 6 eggs (hard-boiled)

- food coloring

- ice

- water

Directions:

1. Add water to 3 bowls, then add different colors of food coloring to each bowl. Mix well.

2. Gently roll the eggs across a hard surface so that their shells get cracks all over.

3. Add 2 eggs to each of the bowls and allow them to sit in the colored water overnight.

4. The next day, drain the water from the bowls and carefully peel off the egg shells to reveal the colored dino eggs.

5. Enjoy!

Frozen Penguins

If you ask all children if they like penguins, they will probably agree. These lovable birds are adorable and interesting, as they use their wings for swimming instead of flying. Here is a simple recipe for frozen penguins made with bananas and chocolates.

Time: 15 minutes (freezing time not included)

Serving Size: 6 servings

Prep Time: 15 minutes

Cook Time: no cooking time

Ingredients:

- 1/2 cup of chocolate (chopped, then melted)
- 3 bananas (peeled, cut in half crosswise)
- 12 edible eyes
- orange frosting

Directions:

1. Tilt the bowl of melted chocolate to one side, then gently dip one of the banana halves into the chocolate. You want to coat the banana half in such a way that the chocolate will look like the black colored of a penguin, and the banana is the white colored part.

2. Place the banana half on a baking tray lined with wax paper, then stick a pair of edible eyes on it.

3. Repeat the coating steps for the rest of the banana halves.

4. Spoon the orange icing into a small plastic bag, then cut off the tip to make a piping bag with a very fine point.

5. Gently pipe small triangles on the faces of the penguins to make the beak.

6. Place the baking tray in the freezer and freeze the banana penguins for about 20 minutes.

7. Serve frozen on a hot summer day.

Chapter 10:

Wrapping Up

Is your mouth watering yet?

Do you feel excited about the recipes you have just read in the previous chapters?

As you can see, cooking with your child doesn't have to be a difficult thing. You can start with simple recipes, then move on to more complex ones once you see that your child has already improved in terms of basic cooking skills like mixing, slicing soft fruits, peeling, measuring, and more. With so many recipes to choose from, you and your child's cooking journey will surely be super fun and exciting!

Recap of Favorite Recipes

Since you have just read so many recipes, you might be feeling a bit overwhelmed. After all, the recipes in this book all sound delicious, don't they? To make it easier for you to choose, why don't you go back to each of the recipe chapters and choose the one that you think would be your favorite? Write one recipe from each chapter, and you will already have a list to start with.

Tips for Continuing the Cooking Journey

Each cooking session you have with your child can become a culinary adventure if you prepare well and try to have fun with your child. Expect things to get messy, especially at the beginning. This is okay. The important thing is to teach your child how to clean up each time they make a mess. Keep doing this until it becomes a habit for them. Aside from this, you can also keep these other tips in mind:

- When assigning cooking tasks to your child, make sure they are age-appropriate. Your child will feel more confident when the skills and tasks you introduce to your child aren't too easy or too difficult. As your child grows older, you can introduce more complex tasks to them.

- The same thing goes when choosing recipes. If this is your first time to cook with your child or if your child is still young, start with simple recipes that won't take a lot of time to make. Doing this will also make your child more engaged in the task instead of getting bored with it.

- Choose a time when you aren't rushing and can focus on the task. Don't worry about waiting around for the food to cook; you can use that time to clean up and explain different things to your child. Cooking when you're in a rush will only make you feel stressed, which might have a negative impact on your child's experience.

- Be patient when cooking with your child. Demonstrate how to perform cooking tasks while explaining in your own words. Always supervise your child until you observe them doing those tasks correctly and on their own.

- Try to make the whole experience fun by having a positive mindset while cooking. Don't expect too much from your child, but give them a lot of chances to show what they can do. And if your child makes a mistake, don't scold them for it. Instead, help them learn from their mistakes.

It's also a nice idea to take a lot of photos while you're cooking with your child. You can also take photos of the dishes you make together and then put together an album to go through to remember everything you've made. Having something like this is a wonderful way to encourage your child to keep cooking.

Encouraging a Lifelong Love for Cooking

The amazing thing about cooking is that you can always learn something new each time you do it. Even if you're the grownup and you're supposed to be teaching your child, you might still discover something new when you cook with your child regularly. Since cooking is an important life skill, helping your child learn this will also benefit them in the long run. So here are some suggestions to help you encourage a love of cooking in your child:

- Make your child feel excited about cooking by pretending that you have a restaurant and you're cooking for your customers. Don't forget to tell the rest of the family to play along too.

- Include your child in planning your family menu. You can even share the recipes in this book with them and ask them to choose which dishes to cook.

- Once in a while, allow your child to think of their own recipes and make those dishes on their own, with your supervision, of course.

- After each cooking session, make sure the whole family eats together to enjoy the food you cooked with your child. Seeing everyone enjoy something they made will definitely put a smile on your child's face.

Keep encouraging your child and giving them positive experiences so that they will always want to keep cooking various dishes with you.

Conclusion:

Start Cooking Now!

Are you ready to start cooking with your child?

Throughout this book, you have learned a wealth of information to help you introduce your child to the wonderful world of cooking. In the beginning of this book, you learned about the benefits of cooking with your child, along with some essential safety tips to keep your child from harm.

Then you discovered the importance of setting up your kitchen to make it easier to teach your child how to cook, including other practical information such as the basic cooking tools that your child would be using and the most common ingredients that you would need in your kitchen.

After learning these fundamentals, all you have to do next is choose one of the recipes from the many chapters in this book. Choose a recipe to start with and go from there. Have fun with the process, and remember to communicate with your child at every step. Soon, you and your child will discover how wonderful it is to cook for yourselves and for the rest of the family.

Happy cooking!

References

Abraham, L. (2018, January 24). *Pizza toast*. Delish. https://www.delish.com/cooking/recipe-ideas/recipes/a57141/pizza-toast-recipe/

Aimee. (2019, January 17). *A stir-fried tofu recipe kids will eat (And love)*. Simple Bites. https://simplebites.net/a-stir-fried-tofu-recipe-kids-will-eat-and-love/

Ainsworth, P. (n.d.). *Fish finger hot dogs*. BBC Good Food. https://www.bbcgoodfood.com/recipes/fish-finger-hot-dogs

Alyssa. (2016, April 29). *Sunset tropical twist sundae recipe*. Arts and Crackers. https://artscrackers.com/2016/04/29/twist-on-the-classic-banana-split/

Arman. (2017, August 7). *Oil free baked veggie chips*. The Big Man's World. https://thebigmansworld.com/oil-free-baked-veggie-chips-paleo-vegan-gluten-free/

Baker, G. (2023, June 8). *30 Essential ingredients every beginner cook needs to have on hand*. Tasting Table. https://www.tastingtable.com/1308478/essential-ingredients-every-beginner-cook-needs-have/

Bauer, E. (2022, February 18). *Kid-friendly wraps*. Simply Recipes. https://www.simplyrecipes.com/recipes/kid_friendly_wraps/

The benefits of including kids in the kitchen. (n.d.). Utah State University. https://extension.usu.edu/healthwellness/research/benefits-of-including-kids-in-the-kitchen

Best, C. (n.d.-a). *Blueberry cheesecake pancakes*. BBC Good Food. https://www.bbcgoodfood.com/recipes/blueberry-cheesecake-pancakes

Best, C. (n.d.-b). *Cookies & cream party cake.* BBC Good Food. https://www.bbcgoodfood.com/recipes/cookies-cream-party-cake

Beth. (2019, May 19). *Veggie snack packs.* Budget Bytes. https://www.budgetbytes.com/veggie-snack-packs/

Betty. (2020a, July 1). *How to make edible dinosaur eggs.* Mombrite. https://www.mombrite.com/edible-dinosaur-eggs/

Betty. (2020b, August 6). *Fluffy 3-Ingredient cloud bread recipe (From TikTok).* Mombrite. https://www.mombrite.com/fluffy-cloud-bread/

Betty Crocker Kitchens . (2010, August 4). *Fruit parfaits.* Betty Crocker. https://www.bettycrocker.com/recipes/fruit-parfaits/2a1f28fe-6977-43c8-a687-042664760b64

BHG Test Kitchen. (2007, February 1). *Peruvian-style chicken tacos.* Better Homes & Gardens. https://www.bhg.com/recipe/chicken/peruvian-style-chicken-tacos/

BHG Test Kitchen. (2020, December 10). *Thai pork shredded tacos with sriracha slaw.* Better Homes & Gardens. https://www.bhg.com/recipe/thai-pork-shredded-tacos-with-sriracha-slaw/

Bond, S. (2018, March 22). *How to set up your kitchen for cooking with toddlers.* Urban Mom Tales. https://urbanmomtales.com/set-up-kitchen-cooking-with-toddlers/

Brandy, E. (2012, March 31). *The basic ingredients you should always have in your kitchen.* Eatwell 101. https://www.eatwell101.com/basic-ingredients-cooking-list-essential-ingredients-cooking

Breakfast sushi recipes for kids. (2022, January 17). Country Home Learning Center. https://countryhomelearningcenter.com/breakfast-sushi-recipes-for-kids/

Brunelli, L. M. (2022, December 6). *Easy pancake recipe for kids*. The Spruce Eats. https://www.thespruceeats.com/kids-can-cook-pancakes-recipe-3542699

Buenfeld, S. (n.d.). *Vegan strawberry pancakes*. BBC Good Food. https://www.bbcgoodfood.com/recipes/vegan-strawberry-pancakes

Butler, T. (2019, June 20). *Creamy 10-Minute beetroot hummus*. The Natural Nurturer. https://thenaturalnurturer.com/the-best-beet-hummus/

Butler, T. (2020a, May 28). *Zucchini and corn fritters*. The Natural Nurturer. https://thenaturalnurturer.com/zucchini-and-corn-fritters/

Butler, T. (2020b, September 22). *Easy lentil veggie quesadillas*. The Natural Nurturer. https://thenaturalnurturer.com/easy-lentil-veggie-quesadillas/

Butler, T. (2021, September 19). *Nut-free school lunch ideas + veggie-loaded pizza rolls*. The Natural Nurturer. https://thenaturalnurturer.com/nut-free-school-lunch-ideas-veggie-loaded-pizza-rolls/

Casner, C. (2023, September 19). *Baked sweet potato curly fries with parmesan*. Eating Well. https://www.eatingwell.com/recipe/274094/baked-sweet-potato-curly-fries-with-parmesan/

Cheese omelette. (2024, January 27). Allrecipes. https://www.allrecipes.com/recipe/262696/cheese-omelette/

Clark, E. (n.d.). *Chocolate chip pancakes*. BBC Good Food. https://www.bbcgoodfood.com/recipes/chocolate-chip-pancakes

Clarke, E. (2015, June 1). *Berry parfait yogurt popsicles*. Well Plated by Erin. https://www.wellplated.com/yogurt-popsicles/

Coles Magazine. (n.d.). *Antipasto mini quiches.* Taste. https://www.taste.com.au/recipes/antipasto-mini-quiches/FsgSzyFv

Cook, D. F. (2023, February 11). *Fantastic fish tacos from kids cook dinner.* Hachette Book Group. https://www.hachettebookgroup.com/storey/fantastic-fish-tacos-from-kids-cook-dinner/

Cooking with kids (For parents). (2021, November). Kids Health. https://kidshealth.org/en/parents/kids-cook.html

Coverdale, K., & Macri , L. (n.d.). *Easy no-bake bunny biscuits.* Taste. https://www.taste.com.au/recipes/easy-no-bake-bunny-biscuits-recipe/v0hh3v2l?r=baking/wuds0hfn

Desmazery, B. (n.d.). *Cooking with kids: Spaghetti & meatballs with hidden veg sauce.* BBC Good Food. https://www.bbcgoodfood.com/recipes/cooking-kids-spaghetti-meatballs-hidden-veg-sauce

Donna. (2017, May 12). *Kids in the kitchen: Yogurt berry parfait.* Whole Food Bellies. https://www.wholefoodbellies.com/yogurt-berry-parfait/

Dulgarian, S. (2018, July 1). *Build your own pizzas (An easy dinner idea).* Somewhat Simple. https://www.somewhatsimple.com/build-your-own-pizzas/

Dunn, J. (n.d.). *Halloween bark.* Good Food. https://www.bbcgoodfood.com/recipes/halloween-bark

Easy 20 Minute chicken tacos. (2019, January 12). Gimme Delicious. https://gimmedelicious.com/chicken-tacos/#recipe

EatingWell Test Kitchen. (2023, September 19). *Kale chips.* Eating Well. https://www.eatingwell.com/recipe/250329/kale-chips/

Emilie. (2014, October 21). *Fruit and veggie turkey: Kid-friendly Thanksgiving snack.* Finding Zest. https://www.findingzest.com/fruit-and-veggie-turkey-kid-friendly-thanksgiving-snack/

European wrap. (2014, August 6). Today's Parent. https://www.todaysparent.com/recipe/snacks/european-wrap-recipe/

5 Ways to get your kids interested in cooking. (2022, October 15). Successful Black Parenting. https://successfulblackparenting.com/2022/10/15/5-ways-to-get-your-kids-interested-in-cooking/

Flory, A. (2019, March 19). *Tips for teaching kids to cook*. Active Kids. https://www.activekids.com/cooking/articles/tips-for-teaching-kids-to-cook

Food Network Kitchen. (n.d.-a). *7 Pancake animals that make breakfast extra fun*. Food Com. https://www.foodnetwork.com/recipes/packages/recipes-for-kids/cooking-with-kids/pancake-animals

Food Network Kitchen. (n.d.-b). *Mac-o-lantern and cheese bowls*. Food Network. https://www.foodnetwork.com/recipes/food-network-kitchen/mac-o-lantern-and-cheese-bowls-3813492

Food Network Magazine. (n.d.). *Chocolate-covered ice cream hearts*. Food Network. https://www.foodnetwork.com/recipes/food-network-kitchen/chocolate-covered-ice-cream-hearts-8046473

Food science experiments. (n.d.). Kids Cooking Activities. https://www.kids-cooking-activities.com/food-science-experiments.html

Fox, K. (2022, January 11). *Cooking with kids: 25+ Recipes to make W with your kids*. Run Wild My Child. https://runwildmychild.com/cooking-with-kids/

Franco, N. (n.d.). *Teach kids to cook for a lifetime of healthy habits*. Bayfront Health. https://www.bayfronthealth.com/content-hub/teach-kids-to-cook-for-a-lifetime-of-healthy-habits

Fuentes, L. (2021, March 3). *Easy avocado salad with Greek yogurt*. MOMables. https://www.momables.com/avocado-egg-salad-sandwich/

Gallagher, S. (2023, January 21). *How to make a yummy omelet recipe for kids with a few ingredients.* The Spruce Eats. https://www.thespruceeats.com/simple-omelette-recipe-for-kids-2098025

Georgy , A. (n.d.). *Cottage pie patties.* Taste. https://www.taste.com.au/recipes/cottage-pie-patties/f616e139-4f76-42a7-8929-41c5904bac16

Gilber, J. (2022, September 22). *Chocolate-dipped ice cream cone cupcakes.* Taste of Home. https://www.tasteofhome.com/recipes/chocolate-dipped-ice-cream-cone-cupcakes/

Good Food Team. (n.d.-a). *Banana ice sundaes with fudge sauce.* Good Food. https://www.bbcgoodfood.com/recipes/banana-ice-sundaes-fudge-sauce

Good Food Team. (n.d.-b). *Creamy ham & mushroom pasta bake.* Good Food. https://www.bbcgoodfood.com/recipes/creamy-ham-mushroom-pasta-bake

Good Food Team. (n.d.-c). *Edible name place biscuits.* Good Food. https://www.bbcgoodfood.com/recipes/edible-name-place-biscuits

Good Food Team. (n.d.-d). *Fruity summer sundaes.* Good Food. https://www.bbcgoodfood.com/recipes/fruity-summer-sundaes

Good Food Team. (n.d.-e). *Pineapple and coconut ice cream sundae.* Good Food. https://www.bbcgoodfood.com/recipes/boozy-pineapple-coconut-sundae

Gray, A. (2017, January 13). *Rainbow fruit parfaits.* Healthy Family Project. https://healthyfamilyproject.com/recipes/rainbow-fruit-parfaits/

Green, D. (2020, October 21). *Best birthday cupcakes.* The Creative Bite. https://www.thecreativebite.com/best-birthday-cupcakes/

Grimes, L. (n.d.-a). *Lunchbox pasta salad*. BBC Good Food. https://www.bbcgoodfood.com/recipes/lunchbox-pasta-salad

Grimes, L. (n.d.-b). *Rainbow pizzas*. BBC Good Food. https://www.bbcgoodfood.com/recipes/rainbow-pizzas

Grow rock candy crystals. (n.d.). Science Buddies. https://www.sciencebuddies.org/stem-activities/rock-candy

Hanka, S. (2021, October 7). *Fully loaded keto breakfast parfait recipe*. Trifecta Nutrition. https://www.trifectanutrition.com/blog/fully-loaded-keto-breakfast-parfait-recipe

Hatem, A. (2021, November 18). *Get your kids excited about cooking with these kitchens toys and tools*. Today. https://www.today.com/shop/cooking-kids-safe-kitchen-tools-t238790

Hebbars Kitchen. (2020, August 13). *Grilled cheese pizza sandwich recipe*. Hebbar's Kitchen. https://hebbarskitchen.com/grilled-cheese-pizza-sandwich-recipe/#google_vignette

Helen. (2016, November 14). *Sticky pork stir fry*. Cooking with My Kids. https://www.cookingwithmykids.co.uk/sticky-soy-and-honey-pork/

Holden, A. (2019, May 23). *Lion pancakes: No special tools required*. Angie Holden the Country Chic Cottage. https://www.thecountrychiccottage.net/lion-pancakes/

Holland, K. (2018, December 6). *Cheesecake cookies recipe*. Southern Living. https://www.southernliving.com/recipes/cheesecake-cookies

How to make your kitchen kid-friendly. (n.d.). Beko Global Ph. https://www.beko.com/ph-en/Blog/healthy-family/how-to-make-your-kitchen-kid-friendly

Huziej, M. (2021, April 29). *Kitchen safety rules for children*. CPD Online College. https://cpdonline.co.uk/knowledge-base/safeguarding/kitchen-safety-rules-for-children/

Itsy Bitsy Foodies. (2013, January 11). *Mr. Baked Potato Heads*. http://itsybitsyfoodies.com/mr-baked-potato-heads/

Jillian. (2014, August 20). *Yogurt parfait breakfast popsicles*. Food Folks and Fun. https://foodfolksandfun.net/yogurt-parfait-breakfast-popsicles/

Johnson, D. (2018, August 22). *Sandwich sushi roll*. Eating Richly. https://eatingrichly.com/sandwich-sushi-roll/

Katerina. (2015, September 30). *Shrimp and broccoli stir fry recipe*. Diethood. https://diethood.com/shrimp-and-broccoli-stir-fry/

Kathlena. (2022, April 22). *Kids sushi recipe: Easy avocado rolls*. Kids Eat in Color. https://kidseatincolor.com/easy-avocado-sushi-roll-recipe/

Katy. (2018, May 18). *Top 7 Kitchen safety kids to teach your kids*. Children's Medical Group. https://childrensmedicalgroup.net/top-7-kitchen-safety-kids-to-teach-your-kids/

Kendrick, S. (2016, May 10). *How to get kids to love cooking*. My Vanderbilt Health. https://my.vanderbilthealth.com/encouraging-a-love-of-cooking-in-your-kids/

Kids beef mini tacos. (n.d.). Old El Paso. https://www.oldelpaso.com.au/recipes/kids-party-mini-tacos-with-beef-and-sweet-potato

Kimball, K. (2019, January 1). *Organizing for a kid-friendly kitchen*. Kids Cook Real Food. https://kidscookrealfood.com/organizing-kid-friendly-kitchen/?affiliate=0

Kitchen safety rules for kids. (n.d.). Blue Flame Kitchen. https://www.atcoblueflamekitchen.com/en-ca/how-to/kitchen-safety-rules-kids.html

Kitchen safety rules for kids. (2021, July 7). UNL Food. https://food.unl.edu/newsletter/food-fun-young-children/kitchen-safety-rules-kids

Korean steak tacos with pickled vegetables. (2015, July 16). Women's Weekly Food. https://www.womensweeklyfood.com.au/recipe/dinner/korean-steak-tacos-with-pickled-vegetables-28880/

Lande, S. (2023, October 26). *12 Kitchen gadgets and tools perfect for kids who love to cook.* Food Network. https://www.foodnetwork.com/how-to/packages/shopping/best-kitchen-knives-and-tools-for-kids

Landis, L. (2018, February 8). *Pantry essentials: Ingredients for a well-stocked kitchen.* Love & Olive Oil. https://www.loveandoliveoil.com/2018/02/pantry-essentials.html

Laura. (2023, January 20). *Best omelette recipe.* Joy Food Sunshine. https://joyfoodsunshine.com/omelette-recipe/

Leih, L. (2023, June 29). *Sloppy joe pasta.* Taste of Home. https://www.tasteofhome.com/recipes/sloppy-joe-pasta/

Lindsay. (2023, April 21). *Nut-free trail mix.* The Lean Green Bean. https://www.theleangreenbean.com/nut-free-trail-mix/

Mack, W. (2021, September 24). *The basic cooking ingredients you should always have.* Kitchen Ambition. https://kitchenambition.com/basic-cooking-ingredients/

Magic mug cake. (n.d.). KiwiCo. https://www.kiwico.com/diy/cooking-baking/treats-dessert/magic-mug-cake

McClelland, S. (2021, May 18). *Easy sorbet recipe.* Little Bins for Little Hands. https://littlebinsforlittlehands.com/how-to-make-sorbet/

McClelland, S. (2022, July 17). *Marshmallow edible slime recipe.* Little Bins for Little Hands. https://littlebinsforlittlehands.com/make-marshmallow-edible-slime-recipe-taste-safe/

Meaney , S. (2024, January 31). *Cooking with children and broadening young palates.* Child Safety Store. https://childsafetystore.com/blogs/news/cooking-with-children-and-broadening-young-palates

Miller, M. (2022, January 6). *Classic Mexican taco recipe (Steps + video!).* How to Cook.Recipes. https://www.howtocook.recipes/classic-mexican-taco-recipe/

Mixer. (n.d.). *Tutti frutti sundae.* World Cancer Research Fund. https://www.wcrf-uk.org/recipes/tutti-frutti-sundae/

Miyashiro, L. (2017a, May 13). *Mac & cheese pizza.* Delish. https://www.delish.com/cooking/recipe-ideas/recipes/a52865/mac-cheese-pizza-recipe/

Miyashiro, L. (2017b, December 1). *Polar bear paw cupcakes.* Delish. https://www.delish.com/cooking/recipe-ideas/recipes/a56687/polar-bear-paw-cupcakes-recipe/

Monson, N. (2023, February 3). *Easy chicken stir fry.* Super Healthy Kids. https://www.superhealthykids.com/easy-weeknight-stir-fry-recipe/

Monster sandwiches. (n.d.). Land O' Frost. https://www.landofrost.com/recipe/monster-sandwiches/

Moore, M. (2021, April 20). *Quick and easy taco cups recipe for kids and adults.* Kitchenatics. https://kitchenatics.com/recipes/taco-cups-recipe-kid-friendly/

Mountford, M. (2011, February 1). *Marshmallow love bugs for Valentine's Day.* The Decorated Cookie. https://thedecoratedcookie.com/marshmallow-love-bugs/

My Kids Lick The Bowl. (2020, May 19). *First birthday cake!* https://mykidslickthebowl.com/1st-birthday-cake/

Nagi. (2023, June 2). *Ham and cheese omelette*. RecipeTin Eats. https://www.recipetineats.com/ham-and-cheese-omelette/

Nagy, K. (2023, April 27). *Free family fun in NYC with food*. Art in the Park 128; Art In The Park 128. https://www.artinthepark128.org/post/family-fun-in-nyc?gclid=EAIaIQobChMIjaSN5OmVhAMV2Tp7Bx2Z3Qy MEAAYASAAEgJv5fD_BwE

Nice, M. (n.d.). *Unicorn cupcakes*. BBC Good Food. https://www.bbcgoodfood.com/recipes/unicorn-cupcakes

Nilsson, H. (2020, February 8). *Valentine's hugs (Pretzel M&Ms)*. Spend with Pennies. https://www.spendwithpennies.com/valentines-hugs/?fbclid=IwAR2L4EPfmr_SX9Nac4rKlxj-Z9DcaxCMp5-tjQfynJbgtUzEC1vWfdbQBn4

Non reader recipes or picture recipes to help cook in the kitchen. (n.d.). Kids Cooking Activities. https://www.kids-cooking-activities.com/non-reader-recipes.html

Nye, J. (2019, August 1). *Trail mix recipe*. I Heart Naptime. https://www.iheartnaptime.net/kids-trail-mix/

Olga. (2018, April 26). *Stress free cooking with kids - Tips to make time Iin the kitchen a good experience for you and your child*. Olga's Flavor Factory. https://www.olgasflavorfactory.com/olgastips/stress-free-cooking-kids-tips-make-time-kitchen-good-experience-child/

Olivier, M. (2023, February 14). *Fruit-filled yogurt parfait (10 Minutes!)*. Baby Foode. https://babyfoode.com/blog/yogurt-parfait/

Palanjian, A. (2021, June 18). *Master trail mix recipe for kids (Easy and healthy)*. Yummy Toddler Food. https://www.yummytoddlerfood.com/trail-mix-recipe/

Pam, & Kalie. (n.d.). *Healthy homemade trail mix kid approved*. Full for Life. https://fullforlife.com/recipe/healthy-homemade-trail-mix-kid-approved/

Pang, M. (2020, August 21). *Essential guide for setting up a kids-friendly kitchen.* LinkedIn. https://www.linkedin.com/pulse/essential-guide-setting-up-kids-friendly-kitchen-maggie-pang?trk=article-ssr-frontend-pulse_more-articles_related-content-card

Parrot Head Mama. (n.d.). *Kiddos favorite trail mix recipe.* Food. https://www.food.com/recipe/kiddos-favorite-trail-mix-100185

Patwal, S. (2015, March 25). *27 Best sandwich recipes for kids.* Mom Junction. https://www.momjunction.com/articles/sandwich-recipes-for-kids_00342426/#cheese-sandwich-recipes-for-kids

Peterson, A. K. (2020, September 8). *Cauliflower-corn tacos with pico verde.* Better Homes & Gardens. https://www.bhg.com/recipe/cauliflower-corn-tacos-with-pico-verde/

Pie maker potato cakes. (n.d.). Kidspot Kitchen. https://www.kidspot.com.au/kitchen/recipes/pie-maker-mashed-potato-cakes-recipe/w28715mw

PureWow Editors. (2018, February 14). *Glazed doughnut cookies.* PureWow. https://www.purewow.com/recipes/glazed-doughnut-cookies-recipe

Quates, J. (2016, March 3). *Easy veggie chips your kids will love.* My Merry Messy Life. https://mymerrymessylife.com/easy-veggie-chips-your-kids-will-love/

Rigg, A. (n.d.). *Snowman cupcakes recipe.* BBC Food. https://www.bbc.co.uk/food/recipes/melting_snowman_cupcakes_77135

Roast pumpkin, tomato and feta pasta. (n.d.). KidSpot Kitchen. https://www.kidspot.com.au/kitchen/recipes/roast-pumpkin-tomato-feta-pasta-recipe/mcy5lfxk

Rose, M. (2022, January 19). *Easy mini pizza recipe for kids.* Design Eat Repeat. https://www.designeatrepeat.com/mini-kids-pizza/

Rossi, S. (2018, January 28). *Chocolate Easter nest cornflake cake recipe.* Taming Twins. https://www.tamingtwins.com/chocolate-easter-nest-cornflake-cake/

Shannon, & Shane. (2012, December 4). *Crafty Christmas snack frozen banana penguin.* Adventures of Our Crazy Life. https://sadlercrazylife.wordpress.com/2012/12/03/crafty-christmas-snack-frozen-banana-penguin/

Sharon. (2013, August 26). *Rainbow tie-dye Swiss roll with strawberry buttercream.* Delishar. http://delishar.com/2013/08/rainbow-tie-dye-swiss-roll-with.html

Shaw, A. (n.d.). *Easy kids' omelette.* BBC Good Food. https://www.bbcgoodfood.com/recipes/kids-omelette

Sindusha. (2015, August 13). *10 Simple sushi recipes for kids.* Mom Junction. https://www.momjunction.com/articles/sushi-recipes-for-kids_00367967/

Stevens, M. (2023, October 20). *Bacon cheeseburger pasta.* Taste of Home. https://www.tasteofhome.com/recipes/bacon-cheeseburger-pasta/

Stewart, M. (2019, January 16). *Confetti cake with vanilla frosting.* Martha Stewart. https://www.marthastewart.com/1514922/confetti-cake-vanilla-frosting

Stewart, M. (2023, May 23). *Triple-chocolate ice cream cake.* Martha Stewart. https://www.marthastewart.com/1531018/triple-chocolate-ice-cream-cake

Sue. (2021, May 4). *Children's cooking utensils: Master list of Montessori cooking tools.* The Montessori-Minded Mom. https://reachformontessori.com/childrens-cooking-utensils/

Tack, K. (2022, October 1). *Eyes on you.* Taste of Home. https://www.tasteofhome.com/recipes/eyes-on-you/

Tasty tacos. (n.d.). KidSpot. https://www.kidspot.com.au/kitchen/recipes/tasty-tacos/8n2h5dga

Thanksgiving turkey cheese ball. (n.d.). Crafts a La Mode. https://www.craftsalamode.com/2015/11/thanksgiving-turkey-cheese-ball.html

Tracy. (2021, April 16). *Blueberry parfait popsicles.* Served from Scratch. https://www.servedfromscratch.com/blueberry-parfait-popsicles/

Travels, T. (2024, May 15). *Froot Loops cereal milk cake.* Florida Milk. https://www.floridamilk.com/in-the-kitchen/recipes/desserts/froot-loops-cereal-milk-cake.stml

Valecha, S. (2024, March 25). *Cooking with kids: 10 Tips to keep it safe and fun.* Heirloom Cookbooks. https://heirloomproject.co/cooking-with-kids-10-tips-to-keep-it-safe-and-fun/

Van, K. (2015, June 9). *Yogurt parfait popsicles.* Lezoe Musings. https://lezoemusings.com/2015/06/09/yogurt-parfait-popsicles/

Vanstone, E. (2020, May 19). *Bake ice cream without it melting!* Science Experiments for Kids. https://www.science-sparks.com/bake-ice-cream-without-it-melting/

Vegetable chips. (2019, October 1). Mimi's Bowl. https://www.mimisbowl.com/baby-and-toddler-recipes/2017/3/24/homemade-vegetable-chips

Wagstaff, L. (2021, June 26). *Easy California sushi roll recipe for kids.* Holidays with Kids. https://holidayswithkids.com.au/california-sushi-roll-recipe/

Wells, M. S. (2019, November 8). *Cathedral window cookies recipe.* Southern Living. https://www.southernliving.com/recipes/cathedral-window-cookies

White, J. (n.d.). *Planet cookies.* BBC Good Food. https://www.bbcgoodfood.com/recipes/planet-cookies

Whiteford, A. (2019, January 17). *The benefits of cooking with kids.* Healthy Little Foodies. https://www.healthylittlefoodies.com/the-benefits-of-cooking-with-kids/

Woodger, L. (2022, May 16). *Easy kids chicken noodle stir fry with broccoli.* The Scatty Mum. https://thescattymum.com/kids-chicken-teriyaki-style-noodles/

Yakkity. (n.d.). *Cheesecake log.* Australia's Best Recipes. https://www.bestrecipes.com.au/recipes/cheesecake-log/ck3hfxcg

Yogurt parfait pops. (2019, May 28). Glitter on a Dime. https://www.glitteronadime.com/yogurt-parfait-pops/

Image References

AndreBeukes. (2021). *Omelette, breakfast, dish.* Pixabay. [Image]. https://pixabay.com/photos/omelette-breakfast-dish-meal-bacon-6600106/

Barbhuiya, T. (2022). *Mix nuts in a bottle.* Pexels. [Image]. https://www.pexels.com/photo/mix-nuts-in-a-bottle-11505597/

Beyers, K. (2019). *Vegetable dish.* Pexels. [Image]. https://www.pexels.com/photo/vegetable-dish-2181151/

Bohovyk, O. (n.d.). *Breakfast cereal bowl with fruits.* Pexels. [Image]. https://www.pexels.com/photo/breakfast-cereal-bowl-with-fruits-7004909/

Briscoe, J. (2019). *Rectangular white tray.* Unsplash. [Image]. https://unsplash.com/photos/rectangular-white-tray-jJDyk_7LXuw

Brown, J. (2018). *Three Cupcakes on white sood.* Unsplash. [Image]. https://unsplash.com/photos/three-cupcakes-on-white-wood-MKBoRZEGeiM

Briscoe, J. (2019). *White over-the-range oven.* Unsplash. [Image]. https://unsplash.com/photos/white-over-the-range-oven-GliaHAJ3_5A

Cegoh. (2016). *Cupcake, dessert, food.* Pixabay. [Image]. https://pixabay.com/photos/cupcakes-dessert-food-muffins-1133146/

Couleur. (2017). Easter eggs basket. Pixabay. [Image]. https://pixabay.com/photos/easter-eggs-basket-easter-eggs-2093315/

Danilevich, O. (2020). *A mother and child mixing a dough.* Pexels. [Image]. https://www.pexels.com/photo/a-mother-and-child-mixing-a-dough-5471928/

Dhinakaran, D. (2023). *An avocado cut in half on a plate.* Unsplash. [Image]. https://unsplash.com/photos/an-avocado-cut-in-half-on-a-plate-77Dsc3nbzEw

Elliot, T. (2020). *White ceramic bowl with brown wooden chopsticks.* Pexels. [Image]. https://www.pexels.com/photo/white-ceramic-bowl-with-brown-wooden-chopsticks-5107162/

Enotovyj. (2018). *A bowl food wood table.* Pixabay. [Image]. https://pixabay.com/photos/a-bowl-food-wood-table-3366480/

Eric X. (2020). *Brown and white pie on white ceramic plate.* Unsplash. [Image]. https://unsplash.com/photos/brown-and-white-pie-on-white-ceramic-plate-BC7iloChihs

EvgeniT. (2019). *Bread bake food flour bakery.* Pixabay. [Image]. https://pixabay.com/photos/bread-bake-food-flour-bakery-4046506/

Fernandes, H. G. (2022). *An egg filled with cheese and mayonnaise.* Pexels. [Image]. https://www.pexels.com/photo/an-egg-filled-with-cheese-and-mayonnaise-11094170/

Freestocks-photos. (2017). *Food, drinks, basil.* Pixabay. [Image]. https://pixabay.com/photos/food-drinks-basil-bowl-cheese-2940358/

Fotomicha. (2015). *Sundae, mandarin sundae, yummy.* Pixabay. [Image]. https://pixabay.com/photos/sundae-mandarin-sundae-yummy-657530/

Gariev, V. (2024). *A woman and a child are making cookies.* Unsplash. [Image]. https://unsplash.com/photos/a-woman-and-a-child-are-making-cookies-SEkjXlYTej0

GC Libraries Creative Tech Lab. (2016). *Shallow focus photography of coffee.* Unsplash. [Image]. https://unsplash.com/photos/shallow-focus-photography-of-coffee-BF0TKHhcuQI

Grey, A. (2018). *Handful of sweet Mexican galletas cookies..* Unsplash. [Image]. https://unsplash.com/photos/baked-cookies-8UHF0HT9Rro

Grey, A. (2020). *Yellow purple and blue textile.* Unsplash. [Image]. https://unsplash.com/photos/yellow-purple-and-blue-textile-BMrL6YDauWE

Gromov, D. (2020). *Blue slushie with white blower.* Unsplash. [Image]. https://www.pexels.com/photo/blue-slushie-with-white-flower-4762722/

Guerita76. (2019). *Tacos, food, chicken.* Pixabay. [Image]. https://pixabay.com/photos/tacos-food-chicken-mexican-4511272/

H, A. (2024). *Plate of chicken tacos with a bowl of dip and lime.* Pexels. [Image]. https://www.pexels.com/photo/plate-of-chicken-tacos-with-a-bowl-of-dip-and-lime-20348820/

Hansel, L. (2020). *Sushi rolls on brown wooden table.* Unsplash. [Image]. https://unsplash.com/photos/sushi-rolls-on-brown-wooden-table-Br3N7xl31fw

Kampus Production. (2021). *Girl holding chopping board with sliced tomatoes.* Pexels. [Image]. https://www.pexels.com/photo/girl-holding-chopping-board-with-sliced-tomatoes-6481570/

Kaboompics, K. (2020). *Close-up of woman holding a glass of yogurt, oats, and fruit.* Pexels. [Image]. https://www.pexels.com/photo/close-up-of-woman-holding-a-glass-with-yogurt-oats-and-fruit-4736076/

Kiser, T. (2017). *Fruit cereal.* Unsplash. [Image]. https://unsplash.com/photos/stainless-steel-spoons-Pw7st6DXLZQ

Lark, B. (2017). *Assorted donuits top of white area.* Unsplash. [Image]. https://unsplash.com/photos/assorted-donuts-top-of-white-area-V4MBq8kue3U

LAWJR. (2017). *Cupcake, dessert, sprinkles.* Pixabay. [Image]. https://pixabay.com/photos/cupcake-dessert-sprinkles-pastry-2250355/

Leman, M. (2021). *Assorted heart-shaped chocolates on Valentine's Day.* Pexels. [Image]. https://www.pexels.com/photo/assorted-heart-shaped-chocolates-on-valentines-day-6765920/

Los Muertos Crew. (2021). *Boy in white shirt and black and red apron sitting on kitchen counter.* Pexels. [Image]. https://www.pexels.com/photo/boy-in-white-shirt-and-black-and-red-apron-sitting-on-kitchen-counter-8064879/

LuckyLife11. (2017). *Sandwich, toast, food.* Pixabay. [Image]. https://pixabay.com/photos/sandwich-toast-food-breakfast-2301387/

Milivigetova. (2015). *Maki, sushi, rice.* Pixabay. [Image]. https://pixabay.com/photos/maki-sushi-rice-avocado-roll-716432/

Monofocus. (2019). *Chia, chia seeds, fresh.* Pixabay. [Image]. https://pixabay.com/photos/chia-chia-seeds-fresh-breakfast-3973466/

Monstera Production. (2020). *Various Halloween gingerbread cookies placed on gray background.* Pexels. [Image]. https://www.pexels.com/photo/various-halloween-gingerbread-cookies-placed-on-gray-background-5635098/

Mukkath, S. (2019). *Veggie pizza on brown wooden tray.* Pexels. [Image]. https://www.pexels.com/photo/veggie-pizza-on-brown-wooden-tray-5640038/

Nasir, M. S. (2021). Brown and white chocolate on white ceramic plate. Unsplash. [Image]. https://unsplash.com/photos/brown-and-white-chocolate-on-white-ceramic-plate-z7Qmxc0rct0

Nemoegluedes. (2015). *Kitchen, omelet, eggs.* Pixabay. [Image]. https://pixabay.com/photos/kitchen-omelet-eggs-food-healthy-775746/

Odintsov, R. (2020). *Quesadillas on a brown wooden board with sliced limes.* Pexels. [Image]. https://www.pexels.com/photo/quesadillas-on-a-brown-wooden-board-with-sliced-limes-4955213/

Olsson, E. (2018). *Assorted fruit and seasoning on table.* Unsplash. [Image]. https://unsplash.com/photos/assorted-fruit-and-seasoning-on-table-I-uYa5P-EgM

Olsson, E. (2019). *Vegetable salad.* Pexels. [Image]. https://www.pexels.com/photo/vegetable-salad-3026808/

Payton, C. (2021). *Spaghetti with meatballs on ceramic plate.* Pexels. [Image]. https://www.pexels.com/photo/spaghetti-with-meatballs-on-ceramic-plate-9617397/

Pexels. (2016). *Berries, muesli, blackberries.* Pixabay. [Image.]. https://pixabay.com/photos/berries-muesli-blackberries-bowl-1846085/

Pixabay. (2014). *Banana cups, bananas, ice cream.* Pixabay. [Image]. https://pixabay.com/photos/banana-cups-bananas-ice-cream-427034/

Rivera, H. (2018). Bowlful of elbow salad. Unsplash. [Image]. https://unsplash.com/photos/bowlful-of-elbow-salad-4qzaeR_sTYA

Shahzad, B. (2020). *Chocolate cake on clear glass plate.* Unsplash. [Image]. https://unsplash.com/photos/chocolate-cake-on-clear-glass-plate-ZCGfYDFm2zQ

Solod_sha. (2021). *Popsicle on a cocktail glass.* Pexels. [Image]. https://www.pexels.com/photo/popsicle-on-a-cocktail-glass-8605710/

StockSnap. (2017). *Pancake, breakfast, food.* Pixabay. [Image]. https://pixabay.com/photos/pancake-breakfast-food-snack-2596104/

Tankilevitch, P. (2020-a). *Fresh sliced vegetables served with sauce in black bowl on tray.* Pexels. [Image]. https://www.pexels.com/photo/fresh-sliced-vegetables-served-with-sauce-in-black-bowl-on-tray-3872351/

Tankilevitch, P. (2020-b). Quiche with cottage cheese. Pexels. [Image]. https://www.pexels.com/photo/quiche-with-cottage-cheese-5419292/

Tafoya, C. (2021). *Person holding white and pink floral ceramic plate.* Unsplash. [Image]. https://unsplash.com/photos/person-holding-white-and-pink-floral-ceramic-plate-hvsGmHIg2U4

Thomas, J. (2020). *Green vegetable on brown soil.* Unsplash. [Image]. https://unsplash.com/photos/green-vegetable-on-brown-soil-z_PfaGzeN9E

Wouter Supardi Salari, . (2021). *White and black dice lot.* Unsplash. [Image]. https://unsplash.com/photos/white-and-black-dice-lot-Euqahx-tMG8

Wikimediaimages. (2017). Candy sugar sweet unhealthy food. Pixabay. [Image]. https://pixabay.com/photos/candy-sugar-sweet-unhealthy-food-2201940/

Yarichev, R. (2020). *Shrimps and vegetables in bowl*. Pexels. [Image]. https://www.pexels.com/photo/shrimps-and-vegetables-in-bowl-17597407/

Yezmin. (2019). Tacos pastor, tacos, tacos Mixco. Pixabay. [Image]. https://pixabay.com/photos/tacos-pastor-tacos-tacos-mexico-4505032/

Zaro, A. (2021). *Brown pastry on white ceramic plate*. Unsplash. [Image]. https://unsplash.com/photos/brown-pastry-on-white-ceramic-plate-iSfIp7k_2Us

Zozz_. (2021). *Donuts, pastries, dessert*. Pixabay. [Image]. https://pixabay.com/photos/donuts-pastries-dessert-glazed-5932003/

Made in United States
Cleveland, OH
29 December 2024

12820812R00179